DUE PROCESS

A Plea for Biblical Justice Among God's People

DUE PROCESS

A Plea for Biblical Justice Among God's People

Daniel C. Juster
Senior Minister: Beth Messiah Congregation
Director: Tikkun Ministries

Destiny Image Publishers
P.O. Box 310
Shippensburg, PA 17257-0310

"Speaking to the Purposes of God for this Generation"

ISBN 1-56043-077-X

For Worldwide Distribution
Printed in the U.S.A.

CONTENTS

FOREWORD

Daniel is right on target in his book, *Due Process*. His thesis could not be more timely—or necessary. Despite the growth of so-called "super churches," apparent numerical growth in general and other quantitative statistics, the influence of the church has been tragically impotent. In fact, if anything, the church has been more and more inculturated by its secular environment so that it is often indistinguishable from the world. In its effort to be "revelant," it has increasingly modified its standards to conform to the world it is attempting to influence.

"Holiness, without which no one will see the Lord..." is no longer sought after. Equipping the laity for ministry has been reduced to programs and methods, rather than "training in righteousness," for which purpose the scriptures were inspired (II Tim. 3:16).

For all practical purposes, the church has ceased to influence the contemporary culture—spiritually, morally or ethically.

Richard C. Halverson
Chaplain, United States Senate

INTRODUCTION

With regards to the American Church at the end of the twentieth century, the words of the prophet certainly hold true: "My people do not understand My ways" (Ps. 95:10; Heb. 3:10). Today, most people who claim to be followers of Jesus do not understand God's standards of righteousness and justice. It is not that we are striving toward that standard and falling short. Rather, we do not even know what our Father expects of us. Our shallow, media Christianity has taught aspects of the basic gospel, but most Christians and Messianic Jews are creatures of shallowness. They have not delved into the Scriptures to understand the ways of God. Popular conceptions of God's ways are at war with the teachings of the Bible. Although the believing community is called to be a city on a hill, a light shining in darkness and the salt of the earth, we are instead a laughingstock of fallen clergy and people full of slander, with children in rebellion. The character of the American Church is at a low ebb and it shortly will be shaken to the core, revealing the foundation of everything in it.

Who am I to make such a statement? Have I been a rabble rouser in the church? No, such is not my nature. My motive stems from a deep love for the many streams of the Body of believers. At twelve years of age I accepted Jesus as Lord and Messiah. Early years of discipleship in an evangelical Reformed Church and in fundamentalist Bible clubs introduced me to people who were sold out to the Lord. I have known many who were the salt of the earth. A godly elder in this Reformed Church was instrumental in leading me into the experience of immersion in the Holy Spirit. At the King's College in Briarcliff Manor, New York, I met godly professors for whom love for the Lord and conformity to His character were more central than academics. I continued to find these characteristics at Wheaton College and at Trinity Evangelical Divinity School. Some, even in these highly academic atmospheres, sought the presence of the Lord, a godly character and a walk with Him more than all other pursuits. My spiritual father at Wheaton, Chaplain Evan Welsh, was the godliest man I have ever known. In love, character and saintliness he was without peer. Our Lutheran pastor in Wheaton, Theodore Laesch, was a servant of great godliness and love. Yes, I have had disappointments in the Church, but my experiences by far have been good. It was through the influence of Chaplain Welsh that I was ordained into the Presbyterian denomination. Providentially, Dr. Welsh was the instrument of my entering into my life's work: seeking to win and nurture those of the house of Israel.

I knew, upon entering the Presbyterian pastorate, that I was entering a denomination that had drifted from its biblical roots. I hoped to be an influence in its return to these roots. Indeed, although not all the emphases in historical Presbyterianism are my "cup of tea," many wonderful and exemplary things can be said for historic Presbyterianism. My taking leadership in the growing Messianic Jewish congregational movement (from 1972 to the present) eventually made my leaving the Presbyterian denomination a practical necessity. These ties were sadly left behind. My desire to identify with the rest of the Body of the Messiah caused me to seek fellowship with groups of leaders who pastored independent charismatic churches.

As part of my responsibilities for the Union of Messianic Jewish Congregations, I was traveling extensively to interdenominational conferences and to churches of all stripes throughout America. It was a great shock to discover the state which many of the churches were in, both locally in my own city and around the country. It was especially so in the charismatic groups to which I most wanted to relate. A "sloppy agape" where almost "anything goes" has become pervasive in the Body of the Lord.

Without standards of righteousness, justice and due process, nothing that is lasting can be built. We will cancel out one another's efforts in competition and mistrust. It will not be long before Satan attacks and sends difficulty. Along with prayer and spiritual warfare, establishing God's standards of righteousness and justice are absolutely essential if the Kingdom of God is to prevail. However, God has promised that His Kingdom will prevail. Therefore I have to believe that His standards will be established again among His people.

My understanding of the Body of believers is a radical one. I believe that we are to be a company of committed people who were soundly converted to the lordship of Jesus. As a result, we are to be a people who have two primary goals in mind. Our first goal is to be conformed to the character and charisma (Holy Spirit life, faith and gifting) of Jesus. Secondly, we are to love the lost, that they might come into a saving relationship with Jesus. Our programs and activities must foster these goals. Out of them issue all other godly goals, including influencing society to righteous standards, reflecting the glory of God in the arts, discovering more about God's world in the sciences and any other worthy goal. However, all is to flow out from a people who consider the pursuit of the first two goals as the way in which they live, move and have their being. The character of Jesus includes the first great godly attitude: to love the Lord God with our all. It is to know Him and make Him known. Biblical liberty is never the right to do as we desire, but a change of our desires so that what we want to do is according to God's holy standard. This change is a product of His life in us. That is true freedom in a biblical sense.

We read of the Messiah that "He will bring forth justice for truth. He will not fail nor be discouraged, till He has established justice in the earth; and the coastlands shall wait for His law" (Isa. 42:3c-4). If what these verses describe is the orientation of Jesus, must it not be ours also? If justice is to be established on the earth, should not the community of His followers be a community of love and justice?

We now turn our attention to answering this question. May the Lord use this modest book in some measure to turn His people toward the godly pursuit of justice. The motive of this endeavor must be love!

CHAPTER I

INJUSTICE AMONG THE PEOPLE OF GOD[1]

Illustration # 1

It was the most blessed fellowship of pastors I had ever been privileged to attend. Ten to fifteen pastors met together weekly. The meeting was simple. Together we worshiped and shared the joys, victories, struggles and disappointments of the ministry. We prayed for one another and the Spirit moved in prophecy to heal, encourage and motivate. Within our fellowship were Presbyterians, Messianic Jews, Methodists, independent Charismatics, charismatic Catholics and some from a recently formed Charismatic Association of Churches. We truly felt love for one another.

After these brothers had met for a year, a new pastor joined the group. Pastor James was leading a newly formed independent charismatic church. During this period, the leader of the pastors' fellowship, Bill Nelms, began to share his love for a charismatic association of churches in the state. He expressed his need for deeper

---

1. Although these accounts are true, the names have been changed for obvious reasons.

commitment of building together beyond the fellowship. He desired to be more intensively related to this organization as well as to be a minister with a relationship to a pastor's fellowship. He invited others who would be interested to investigate this association. He assured the group that he loved the pastors' fellowship and would continue in his commitment to it. The fellowship was assured that he was not seeking to make the fellowship part of this charismatic association, for he understood that others had different denominational ties and other associations. However, it was possible that a local expression of this association might root itself in the county if others followed him into this commitment.

Most of the brothers received his sharing graciously and were supportive. However, Pastor James raised his suspicions and mistrust for that association of churches. Indeed, at a later meeting he brought another pastor friend who had not had any relationship to the weekly fellowship. This pastor, Pastor Jacobs, was extremely antagonistic to the association of churches that the fellowship leader sought to join. Pastor Jacobs claimed to have had bad experiences with the leader of this association of churches and with another association of churches that related to the first. They were all into "the shepherding movement," he asserted. He also claimed to sense a hidden agenda in the motives of Pastor Nelms, the fellowship leader.

Many accusations were made; some answers were offered. However, the agenda of the devil was fulfilled. Such mistrust was spread that the group never recovered. The weekly, county pastors' fellowship would never be the same. Attendance dropped off; the spirit just was not the same. We were all sad.

Many accusations were made, but how should they be judged? Pastor Jacobs led one of the leading charismatic churches in the area at that time. Many believed him. However, the groups that were charged had no day in court to respond. There was no fair judiciary to hear the evidence and render a judgment or bring peace. A wounded spirit or an unhealed hurt certainly motivated Pastor Jacobs when he forcefully put forth his accusations. Yet there was no unity in standards of covenant behavior, justice or due process among the pastors of the fellowship. It was a fatal weakness from which the group would not recover. Satan found our Achilles heel and the fellowship died.

Illustration # 2

A monthly, county-wide pastors' fellowship also existed. By default, I became the leader of this fellowship. It did not have quite the spirit and power of the other, but brothers still found encouragement from being together. This fellowship met monthly and included a denominational mix similar to the one described previously, as well as some Assemblies of God pastors from the area.

One of the churches in the area had undergone a major leadership crisis. Pastor Wilkens of this church had been caught in a homosexual tryst. The two involved had not "gone all the way," according to their testimony. Pastor Wilkens professed repentance. However, during the application of discipline, he brought many accusations against the leadership of this church. Eventually he was removed from leadership, and found himself in a process that was leading to his disfellowshipping. During this time, he allegedly spread his accusations to many others in the church.

To handle this difficult situation, the leaders of New Hope Church submitted themselves to seven national leaders. These seven leaders confirmed the discipline of the church. Coincident with Pastor Wilkens' removal from all leadership, they advised him to receive restoration in a congregation in another state from whose ranks one of the seven came. The discipline was agreed to by all.

However, after some time had elapsed, Pastor Wilkens claimed he could not sell his house. He took that as a sign from God. He also maintained that he never was given the opportunity to present his case before the counsel of seven. Indeed, he declared that the principles of due process were severely violated. Furthermore, he insisted that the real issue was the leadership structure of this church and its abusive authority. He claimed to be pursuing this issue before the sexual fall. I doubt that the inability to sell his house was a sign from God. As the old real estate adage proclaims, any house will sell if the price is low enough and the basement is dry. This leader's non-compliance with the directives for restoration and his continued spreading of accusations caused the church to disfellowship him.

Pastor Wilkens then proceeded to go and see Pastor Jacobs, whose church was a few miles down the road. Pastor Jacobs had major disagreements and bitterness toward the other leaders of New Hope Church. After a brief period of counsel, he (with the involvement of other pastors) declared Pastor Wilkens restored. Shortly afterwards, Pastor Wilkens started a new church in the same area as New Hope Church.

Soon Pastor Wilkens showed up at the monthly pastors' fellowship. The leaders of New Hope Church stood up to excuse themselves; they explained that they could not, in good conscience, sit in fellowship with a person who was disfellowshipped. However, I as the leader of the fellowship simply couldn't allow that to happen. I therefore asked Pastor Wilkens to leave.

After his departure, an impassioned discussion began concerning the disfellowshipping that had taken place. The questions were many. Some were concerned that local pastors did not confirm the disfellowshipping, although it affected them. Also, why were seven leaders from around the country chosen, and not seven local leaders? (It later was suggested that a local council of leaders who believe in discipline should have an opportunity to confirm the decision. After all, it was argued, it was a matter that would primarily continue to effect the church in the local area. The disfellowshipped leader was willing for such a court to be convened. However, the elders of the New Hope Church were not willing to review the case again.)

Others voiced the concern that our meeting was "just a pastors' fellowship" and should have nothing to do with enforcing discipline. (This statement implies that no standards exist for those who attend pastors' fellowships.) Even the Assemblies pastors could not see how it was right to ask Pastor Wilkens to leave the fellowship. The Assemblies brothers admitted that, in their own denomination, there was usually a two-year restoration period in cases of discipline for significant sexual sin, but that it did not apply to a pastors' fellowship. Others agreed with my decision; the leaders from New Hope Church argued that not only was the disfellowshipping valid, but also that a pastors' fellowship should uphold such discipline. What was the result of this debate? The destruction of pastors' fellowship number two!

Those who did not believe in enforcing standards in a pastors' fellowship in general, or at least in this case, did not want to come if the individual involved was excluded. Furthermore, they gave credibility to Pastor

Jacobs of the large charismatic church. He declared this disfellowshipping invalid and, with others, recommissioned Pastor Wilkens. Some of the others in the monthly group who wanted to enforce standards lost their heart for pastors' fellowships and decided to simply stay within their own circles. Interestingly enough, Pastor Jacobs had a difficult marriage and family life. He was later removed from his church for gross sexual immorality. Did his own moral weakness influence his attitude toward discipline and restoration?

Another fellowship was dead. Those few who did not lose heart and did want to uphold standards no longer were able to gather support. The charismatic congregations of the county drifted apart with little fellowship or joint cooperation. Again there was no agreement, unity in standards or due process that the leaders could apply to settle the issues among us.

Illustration # 3

As president of our national association of congregations, I was asked to resolve a situation where one congregation had split into two. During this meeting I found that Pastor Simms of Congregation Hope of Israel was separated from his wife and was seeing his secretary. Questioning led to the discovery of a pattern of sexual sin. I found that the pastor's marriage had been very difficult all along. That was the occasion of falling.

Why didn't the elders remove him from leadership? The reason was twofold. First, they claimed that he was very intimidating, manipulative and persuasive concerning his call, anointing and the probable, negative results of his removal. Secondly, he established a constitution and by-laws whereby he could not be removed. His power in the corporation was absolute. He had copied this form of government from the Praise of Israel Congregation in another city. The leaders of Praise of Israel had spread far and wide the teaching on the rightness of this form of government. (Few were willing to take a strong public stand against this teaching in our movement.)

Our only alternative was to remove him and his group from the association. (He later did divorce his wife and marry his secretary.) We received the remaining group, with its new name of Messiah Fellowship, into the association after exhorting the leaders that they should have been stronger in confrontation, in spite of the by-laws.

As a result of this situation, one of the larger congregations in our association was now defunct; few of the people continued with the new group, Messiah Fellowship. People were too demoralized. Eventually, Pastor Simms sold the building of Hope of Israel Congregation and put the money in the bank. He could now do ministry by living off the interest. He now had an endowed ministry!

Illustration # 4

Another leading pastor and teacher, James Scott, divorced his wife and married his secretary. The churches he led disfellowshipped him, for they claimed he did not have biblical grounds for divorce. Soon afterwards he came to our area and found a platform on a Christian radio station. Several pastors in the area protested, only to be told that radio was a broad Christian forum with no authority to enforce discipline. Pastors in the area, myself included, sought direct testimony from the churches involved in the disfellowshipping. Was it valid? A spokesman from these churches claimed that although the marriage was difficult, and although there were problems on both sides (perhaps the wife was the bigger problem), before the divorce occurred, the wife had been willing to seek reconciliation and counsel toward a good marriage. We were told that Pastor Scott had been unwilling. In their clear and firm conviction, he did not have biblical grounds for divorce and remarriage.

Today James Scott is received as a major speaker throughout much of the charismatic movement. We are told, "He repented of his sin; indeed, we are all sinners saved by grace. It is not ours to judge." Yet we know of no repentance in these words: "I was wrong to divorce and remarry as I did; were I to have it to do over, I would desire to not sin against my Lord in this way. I step down from ministry for restoration. My new marriage is, however, my present responsibility."

In today's charismatic movement, divorce and remarriage, without biblical grounds as classically understood, is permitted. If one simply is willing to tough it out and maintain the ministry, and is an attractive personality or forceful orator, acceptance will follow! There need be no process of restoration. As one prominent leader told me, to my great shock, "Who are we to judge? We are to act in love. Only God can judge and know when restoration has taken place, whether it is in a day or a year. If there is fruitfulness in the ministry, obviously God has restored."

However, how do we measure fruitfulness? Is it in the size of the ministry? Is it the number of souls saved? How will our children respond? What will become of our children's values and their perseverance through conflict when they see such examples? As one young teen asked, "Dad, is divorce okay with God?" Thank God she asked. Many of our impressionable youth simply will assume that it is so. Conflict in a marriage is, in itself, not grounds for divorce and remarriage.

Illustration # 5

A leading media televangelist, Jacob Gardiner, fell into sexual sin. He was part of a denomination that maintained standards for repentance and restoration. He had pledged in his ordination vows that, if he sinned in this way, he would disclose it and submit to the standards of the denomination. Before his fall, Evangelist Gardiner was sharply and publicly critical of other ministries. There was no due process in the accusations he brought forth. Soon after the denomination made its decision on the process and time of restoration required for him, Jacob Gardiner left the denomination and resumed his ministry. What about his pledge to the standards of the denomination? The Christian public is told, "We are to forgive and not judge. We are all sinners saved by grace." However, is that really the meaning of not judging? Does forgiveness mean that there is no process of restoration under human undershepherds?

Illustration # 6

Recently word has been passed through the charismatic grapevine that the leader of a major association of congregations, Rev. Howard Johnson, has been in long-term, repeated adultery. However, those to whom this minister looks for accountability simply slapped his wrists, told him to stop his adultery and allowed him to continue in his ministry. Some who are part of this association have spread this report. They are greatly disappointed.

How should the Body of the Messiah respond to this association, its leader and those to whom he is accountable? On the other hand, are the ministers in this association and others outside it justified in spreading this report? Have they followed biblical standards in going to

the minister and to others in charge? Indeed, should
they by such a process try to see that a group of leaders
hears the evidence and renders a decision regarding the
minister (and even his authorities)? To not do so and to
repeat the charges is to spread hearsay. After all, how do
we know that the report is really true?

There is widespread mistrust in the Body of the Messiah concerning the leaders involved and their association. Some counsel that we are to forgive. After all,
"Love believes all things." Only God can judge, we are
told. Yet is this really what the Bible teaches?

Illustration # 7

Recently Pastor Dan Jarvis was approached by a
friend concerning Pastor Jarvis' informal relationship
with a prominent national leader, Rev. David Spock. He
was told by this friend that David Spock was untrustwor-
thy and had been judged by his former denomination
for gross immorality, from which he never repented. It
was said that David Spock responded to the discipline by
leaving the denomination and starting his own movement. When he approached the leaders of the denomination, Pastor Jarvis found that there was no official
decision concerning Rev. Spock that they were willing to
disclose. They only would state that they neither sup-
ported nor opposed his ministry. Should Pastor Jarvis
separate from Rev. Spock on the basis of this report?
Should he doubt Pastor Spock? Is the denomination's
stance correct if they really had clear evidence of gross
moral sin?

During the course of the conversation, the friend also
reported an incident that happened thirty years earlier
and involved another leader. According to a reliable
report, Evangelist Jack Bixler, who was married at the

time, was caught in bed with another woman. Other prominent leaders knew of it and since that time would have nothing to do with him. Yet there was no record of evidence, discipline, repentance or restoration of any kind. How should Pastor Jarvis respond to this report?

Illustration # 8

Rev. Sam Greenwald was part of a loose association of congregations. He reported to the executives of this association that his second wife had left him. The executives of the association advised him that although it appeared from his report that his wife abandoned the marriage (they had not yet had an opportunity to talk to the wife), under the circumstances, it would be best for him to step down from the ministry and to look for another leader for the congregation. The executives made it clear that they could not require him to do so under the present standards of the association, but it would be best. Soon afterwards Pastor Greenwald left this association and joined another association that was acting in great competition toward the first group. They proceeded to make Pastor Greenwald a national figure! Pastor Greenwald brought into his new association many bad reports of the leaders of his former association. His reports were fully received and spread by the leaders of his new association.

Illustration # 9

A leader of an association of congregations was publicly accused of false theology and divisive behavior by leaders in another association. Despite the lack of a fair hearing of the evidence or any due process, many were affected by these reports. Others who knew these reports to be groundless continued to support the accusing leadership.

These people reasoned that it was not their battle, that they were not to take up an offense and that their continued support of the accusing leaders was a demonstration of love which could bring change. Are these correct interpretations of biblical norms (love, not taking up a bad report)? What of justice? We are told, "Justice is the Lord's. He will bring it! It is not our concern."

Illustration # 10

A pastoral leader in a local congregation falls into sexual sin after becoming "burned out" in ministry. Rev. John Spaith steps down from ministry under the direction of leadership friends who are called in to provide guidance. After the requisite time of restoration has passed, the fallen leader seeks to be restored. His friends, however, perceive a different eldership calling for his life. This causes a split in the congregation. The majority asks Rev. Spaith to resume his pastoral role among them. Although the discipline of restoration was obeyed, the grounds for his stepping down were not made public. It was thought best to keep the grounds private in order to protect the man and his family.

Six years later, a split ensues between this leader and others in his congregation. Elder Bill Parish, who served as an elder before the discipline took place, knew of the situation that called for the discipline. Now six years after that situation, he brings forth many accusations in a lengthy letter, mixing the old sins with new accusations. Bill Parish, the accuser, is himself in adultery and is eventually disfellowshipped! Great doubt, however, has spread concerning Pastor Spaith.

Did the authorities who brought discipline six years earlier handle it properly? Should discipline be private, if at all possible, in these situations?

Illustration # 11

A prominent leader of a large church sends out a manuscript and tapes with serious accusations against another group of leaders which oversees a large community in the same city. Pastor Jack Clements claims to have approached the leaders of this community without good results. He accuses them of prophesying falsely, teaching gross false doctrine and prophesying by familiar spirits. These accusations cause divisions in many congregations that have established relationships with the accused leaders. Although a claim was made that Matthew 18 was followed, according to the accused leaders, that is not the case. Indeed, Pastor Clements never called a council of elders to hear the evidence or a joint eldership from both groups to hear the concerns.

Finally, another minister, Samuel Leslie, investigates the charges. He finds significant areas for correction, but does not substantiate any of the charges of gross doctrinal error, gross abuse of prophecy, use of familiar spirits in prophesying or gross misrepresentation. Pastor Clements withdraws some of his accusations after this investigation, and even states that his grave accusations against one prophetic leader were based on false evidence! Yet the accusations still are spread throughout the Body of the Messiah. Pastor Clements still claims that most of his accusations remain valid. How should this situation be handled?

The American Church in 1990

The previous examples are only a small sampling. I wish I could say that this small sampling is exceptional. It is not. It is true that there are many good and moral leaders who seek to serve the Kingdom of God with holiness and devotion. However, even within this group there is confusion concerning the issues of government and discipline. We would not find a consensus on how these situations should be handled. The Body of the Messiah in America is beset by several problems.

First of all, we have the myths of wrong theology. Among these is the major falsehood of our day which I call "sloppy agape." Under this term I put all of the teaching that says love and forgiveness require us to forego seeing justice in the Body of the Messiah. Not only is it not believed that the Church should be a just society in the midst of a perverse world, justice is perceived as a lower Old Testament standard contrary to New Testament grace. The concepts of non-judgmentalism and forgiveness have produced an "anything goes" mentality in the Church.

Secondly, we have fragmentation among Bible believers. There are many scores of denominations and associations. The number of these groups would not be so bad if these associations were related together and respected some common standards of righteousness and justice. However, there is such mistrust between so many of these groups that discipline in one group holds no weight with the others. A plethora of groups and associations would not be bad if they were mutually supportive and cooperative on issues of basic standards and ethical behavior.

However, in North America we like our freedom. In religious circles that means the right to hang up a shingle and start ministries. This is easier than securing a Small Business Administration loan to start a new company. Many leaders see today's church as entrepreneurial and competitive. There is no consensus on leadership standards for experience, training or character. Even within associations, discipline is sometimes difficult to enforce. Many in the charismatic world have left the mainline denominational world. Because the latter has largely apostatized, the charismatic groups reject all that is within the denominational world, even the historic standards of due process forged through hard experience in the earlier days of the denomination's faithfulness!

In the mainline denominational world, true belief in the Scriptures is only found in a minority. The classic standards of the denomination are rarely applied. For example, the Book of Order of the Presbyterian Church was a textbook in our seminary days in 1972. I was awed by the wisdom in this manual. During the class on polity, I asked the professor if she knew of any church that had applied its standards and process for excommunication. For me as an evangelical, the response was amazing. She noted that it was very rare to see them applied today. However, there was one case where a Sunday school teacher was disfellowshipped because he refused to stop teaching the Genesis creation accounts as literal and would not submit to the church's view that these were symbolic accounts which should be squared with the theory of evolution.

A comparison of the late nineteenth century evangelical church with the late twentieth century charismatic and evangelical churches (despite areas of restored truth) reveals an enormous decline in America in several areas: ethical standards for those in ministry leadership; standards for church membership; accountability for church leadership; the process of discipline for members and leaders and the general condition of holiness. We in America are seeing the lowest standards among non-Catholics since Luther railed against the abuses and immorality in the Catholic church.

Is the role of the Church completely different from the role of Israel? It was God's desire that it would be

said of Israel, "What nation is there that has a God so
near and a law so just as all this law," which God gave
through Moses (See Deutronomy 4:7-8). God is a God of
love, but God's love must be compatible with seeking justice. Because Israel fell from God's standards of morality
and justice, we read that the Name of God was blasphemed among the nations. Yet it was God's intention
that godliness and justice would characterize Israel. That
was her witness to the truth.

Is there not a parallel role for the Church? Are the
promises of God experienced so little because of the lack
of holiness, righteousness and justice within our ranks?
Are there biblical ethical standards to be enforced
among those who claim to be members of the Messiah's
Body? Are there biblical standards for leaders to be enforced? Is there due process for dealing with sin, disputes and accusations? Is it required by Scripture? How
does love and forgiveness square with God's injunction
in the prophets that we are to seek justice or with the
fact that God says righteousness and justice are the *foundation* of His throne? Is the recent editorial in a leading
Christian magazine correct when it undercut church discipline by claiming that only God is to judge the heart?
May God lead us as we deal with these and other questions in the next chapters.

CHAPTER II

JUSTICE AND THE HEBREW SCRIPTURES

What implications do the Hebrew Scriptures have concerning the issue of justice and due process for the Body of believers today? First of all, we assume in this chapter that the basic thrust of the Hebrew Scriptures is valid for the New Covenant age.

The church today lives in an abysmal vacuum concerning the issues of ethics and justice. The New Testament assumes the teaching of the Hebrew Scriptures on these issues. It does not repeat much of its content, but makes a clear statement of its relevance (II Tim. 3:16-17). That God is a God of love, mercy and justice is all of one fabric in the Hebrew Scriptures; hence the relevance of a book like Walter Kaiser's *Toward an Old Testament Ethic*. Kaiser did not mean to write only for understanding ethics in the Old Testament period, but also that the ethics of the Hebrew Scriptures should be applied today! Yet many do not teach the ethics of the Bible, fearing that such teaching is too restrictive for twentieth century people!

The Hebrew Scriptures present God as a God who loves justice and who expects His people to pursue it. That is our first thesis. Our second thesis is that God established Israel to reflect the superiority of life under

God's rule, a life under His principles of ethics and justice. Our last thesis is that the order of life prescribed for ancient Israel in the Hebrew Scriptures was an order in which no individual, family, leader, city or clan was to be beyond accountability. This implies a means to pursue justice under human officials. Justice is not merely something God will bring, but something that human beings are commanded to pursue.

In the Hebrew Scriptures, justice and love are not opposites. It is impossible, in this perspective, to seek love without justice. To practice, permit or allow injustice is to destroy love. An unjust society is characterized by trampling upon others, the opposite of loving our neighbors as ourselves. Following the order of justice under the laws of God produces in a society the highest fulfillment and harmony between human beings. Mercy may be offered for the truly repentant, but the unrepentant are to be brought to justice! The Hebrew Scriptures constantly enjoin the rulers to give themselves to righteousness by bringing justice! The solution to the human miscarriage of justice is not to do away with the process of judgment, but to bring this process under the standard of God through godly judges!

What is justice? It is simply God's righteous order for humanity. It is life under his rule. It is not humanistic equality where differences of gifts, roles, wealth and calling are eliminated. It is equality before the courts. There *are* mandates for economic *opportunity*. Our prayer for the coming of God's kingdom is a prayer for Him to establish his loving, righteous rule in our midst.

The Torah: God's Standard for Love, Justice and Mercy

Before we continue by taking a brief look at the Torah (the writings of Moses), we cannot too strongly emphasize that the biblical concept of justice is not the same as the humanistic one. In secular humanism, justice often means equality in the sense of sameness. It is a concept that leads to socialism. Justice, for example, would mean equality of income for all people (and a huge centralized bureaucracy to enforce it). Biblical justice, on the other hand, allows for differences in calling, income, wealth and gifting. However, biblical justice establishes rules for opportunity whereby no class can perpetually control all wealth in a way that suppresses the poor. Opportunity, for example, is provided by the redistribution of land every fifty years and the canceling of debts every seven years. Also, a person's faith, diligence, generosity and creativity were allowed to flourish.

Justice in the Scriptures is inclusive of the following concepts. First is equality before the Law of God. Those who break a law or who have a case at law against another, whether they be rich or poor, are entitled to swift and fair justice before godly judges. Secondly, justice is defined by God's standards for human relations. To act justly and lovingly is not indulgence or an application of some sociological theory whereby the criminal is coddled. Rather, justice and love are defined by acting according to the law. Love includes an attitude of compassion toward our fellow man that seeks his highest good.

The highest good and fulfillment for man is to live in *loving fellowship* with God and man. However, biblical love does not overlook gross sin, even if the sinner is one's own kin. Even the closest relative is to be brought to justice by his kin for the sake of love and faithfulness to God. The highest good can be fulfilled only by living in accord with the Law of God, for His Law is the pattern that enables fulfillment. Yielding to behavior contrary to God's Law destroys love and community. The broken law exacts a penalty whether by society and its judges or by God's intervention. There is also a blood sacrifice that can bring forgiveness for many offenses. All have sinned, and all must sacrifice. Gross rebellion and its manifest acts must be punished according to the penalties of the law. To not punish sin is to leave a corporate stain on the community and to bring the whole community under the judgment of God. The Bible teaches that the influence of upbringing is important. The Bible speaks in corporate terms. Yet it still requires right behavior from every individual.

For the Torah, justice is impossible for man unless all judges serve under the ultimate Lawgiver and Judge, the Creator of heaven and earth. Thus the law begins with the words, "I am the LORD your God, who brought you out of the land of Egypt, out of the house of bondage" (Ex. 20:2). Love, loyalty and gratitude toward God are the chief motives for the pursuit of justice. Fear of penalty is a secondary motive. In the Ten Commandments, we read that God is merciful and just!

> ...*For I, the* LORD *your God, am a jealous God, visiting the iniquity of the fathers on the children to the third and fourth generations of those who hate Me, but showing mercy to thousands, to those who love Me and keep My commandments.*
>
> Exodus 20:5-6

Chapters 21 through 23 of Exodus provide the guidelines for the judges who are to be appointed in every town. Chapter 21 opens with the words, "Now these are the judgments which you shall set before them."

There are laws concerning servants, murder, animal control, property rights and more. There are laws for family life and marital purity. Sexual intercourse outside of marriage gave the father of the girl the right to require the couple to make the commitment of marriage. Adultery, bestiality and homosexuality were punished by death.

Justice in our speech toward one another is a crucial standard of covenant. Its violation brought severe penalties.

> *You shall not circulate a false report. Do not put your hand with the wicked to be an unrighteous witness. You shall not follow a crowd to do evil; nor shall you testify in a dispute so as to turn aside after many to pervert justice.... Keep yourself far from a false matter; do not kill the innocent and righteous.... And you shall take no bribe, for a bribe blinds the discerning and perverts the words of the righteous.*
>
> Exodus 23:1-2; 7-8

A bribe with money is one type; but how much justice is foregone in the Body of believers because of stroking, offering status and other more subtle types of bribery?

It is my desire that we concentrate on the issue of gross slander and character assassination that is so prevalent in the Body today. This problem is intensified because there often is no process to handle significant accusations. The Torah enjoins that all cases must be decided on the basis of real evidence (in the mouth of two or three witnesses). We read, "You shall not go about as a talebearer among your people; nor shall you take a stand against the life of your neighbor: I am the LORD" (Lev. 19:16). The same Torah, however, requires us to correct and rebuke a neighbor! To not do so is to hate him (Lev. 19:17). Because Israel required judicial action where there was gross sin, anyone who falsely accused another of gross sin could be brought to court and suffer the judicial penalty of that sin.

*And the judges shall make a diligent inquiry, and in-
deed, if the witness is a false witness, who has testified
falsely against his brother, then you shall do to him as
he thought to have done to his brother; so you shall put
away the evil person from among you. And those who
remain shall hear and fear, and hereafter they shall not
again commit such evil among you.*

Deuteronomy 19:18-20

Gross slander is serious business in the Hebrew Scriptures. According to Proverbs 6:17, a false witness who
pours out lies commits one of the seven sins most detest-
able to the Lord. There must be a just means of dealing
with situations of gross slander and gossip which bring
discord and separate brothers.

The Torah contains laws on showing kindness to the
poor, on treating the stranger with kindness, on in-
heritance and much more. Great emphasis is put on
respect for authority. This is especially so with regard to
family life. A son who curses his father or mother is to be
put to death, according to Scripture (Ex. 20:17; Lev.
20:9). We read also that "Every one of you shall revere
his mother and his father" (Lev. 19:3a).

In no way can this small book deal with all of the laws
of God in the Torah. However, the Law of God can be
summarized by the principle of loving God with our all
and our neighbor as ourselves. The stranger is included
as one to be so loved. Therefore, the Torah enjoins
equal treatment before the courts for all people; it enjoins just weights and measures in all business dealings
and fair wages so that the poor are not oppressed! The
workers are to share in the profits of the enterprise.

Appointing Judges

Not all of the laws of the Torah can be enforced.
Some are for personal guidance. However, many of the

laws of God can be enforced. How are the laws to be enforced when specific infractions can be proved by material evidence or testimony? The answer is in Israel's judicial system. Israel established a system of checks and balances among prophets, priests and civil rulers. All were accountable to God. At this point we will emphasize the judges. In Deuteronomy 16, we read:

> *You shall appoint judges and officers in all your gates, which the* LORD *your God gives you, according to your tribes, and they shall judge the people with just judgment. You shall not pervert justice; you shall not show partiality, nor take a bribe, for a bribe blinds the eyes of the wise and twists the words of the righteous. You shall follow what is altogether just, that you may live and inherit the land which the* LORD *your God is giving you.* (vv. 18-20)

The Torah repeatedly emphasizes that the courts are especially to respect the legal rights of the poor, the fatherless and the widow (Deut. 10:18). It is far too easy for the powerful to exploit or oppress them and to break the laws of God. Although judges must not show partiality to the poor if they commit crimes, the judges are to especially see that might does not make right in Israel.

The gates were the places of judgment in each village. A village would have a population ranging from a few hundred to a few thousand people. Every village had its judges. Most individuals were to deal with the concerns in the local village. For cases that were too difficult, there was an appeal structure.

> *If a matter arises which is too hard for you to judge, between degrees of bloodguiltiness, between one judgment or another, or between one punishment or another, matters of controversy within your gates, then you shall arise and go up to the place which the* LORD *your God*

chooses, and you shall come to the priests, the Levites, and to the judge there in those days, and inquire of them; they shall pronounce upon you the sentence of judgment. You shall do according to the sentence which they pronounce upon you in that place which the LORD *chooses. And you shall be careful to do according to all they order you. ...you shall not turn aside to the right hand or to the left from the sentence which they pronounce upon you.*

Deuteronomy 17:8-11

Those who would depart from such judgment were to be put to death!

No One Is Beyond Accountability

The structure of government in ancient Israel was a decentralized structure of judge-governors over towns and tribes. There was an appeal to the highest court in Jerusalem. In First Samuel we read of God's great concern for Israel because of her desire for a king. However, if Israel chose a king, even this king was not above the law. That is amazing in the context of the ancient Near East. In the surrounding lands the king was the law! In Israel we are told that the king was to make himself a copy of the law (Deuteronomy) and to observe all of it so that "his heart may not be lifted above his brethren, that he may not turn aside from the commandment..." (Deut. 17:20). There is nothing to indicate that the removal of the king was precluded. The process for removal is not clearly stated. Perhaps the supreme court and the leading judges could bring judgment against him if he grossly violated the law. Israel often fell to such a degree that the people followed the sinful kings. *God did raise up others with the authority to depose sinful kings.* (Such was the case with Jehu.) The prophetic office was used to bring rebuke. Sometimes the prophetic word would lead to the king's replacement in a coup.

There was even a process to deal with a village or city in gross violation of God's Law. Could that be parallel to congregations and organizations? In Deuteronomy 13:12-18 we read that the cities of Israel were to rise up and strike a rebellious and idolatrous city. Gross sin occurred in Gibeah in Judges 19. Because the Benjamites did not stand for justice in this situation, but protected Gibeah, the whole tribe was punished by the rest of Israel. Justice clearly must be applied to corporate situations of tribes, cities and families.

Deuteronomy 17:11-12 teaches the importance of respecting the decisions of the judges. The judges act in a God-appointed capacity and represent His justice. Therefore, contempt for the judges leads to the death penalty. All individuals are to agree with the decision of the judges so that there might be an enforcing of justice.

God's intention for Israel as a just and loving society was related to the concept of witnessing and turning the nations back to God. To Israel, He says:

And now, Israel, what does the LORD your God require of you, but to fear the LORD your God, to walk in all His ways, and to love Him, to serve the LORD your God with all your heart and with all your soul, and to keep the commandments of the LORD and His statutes which I command you today for your good?

Deuteronomy 10:12-13

If the Israelites walk in the ways of God, they will have long life and be protected from disease (Deut. 7:15). We read that the nations will thereby gain an understanding of God's truth.

...for this is your wisdom and your understanding in the sight of the peoples who will hear all these statutes, and

say, "Surely this great nation is a wise and under-standing people." For what great nation is there that has God so near to it, as the LORD our God is to us, for whatever reason we may call upon Him? And what great nation is there that has such statutes and righteous judgments as are in all this law which I set before you this day?

Deuteronomy 4:6-8

The severe violation of God's standards brought great judgment upon the nation of Israel. Israel was not, through most of her history, the model of a just and loving society. Idolatry and injustice came together in ancient Israel.

It is well to ask some important questions. Does the teaching of the Torah have relevance for the issue of justice in today's church? Is the Body of believers a just society? Are leaders and people to be accountable to judges in a fair process that considers evidence and testimony when there is gross sin or a significant dispute? Should there be a means for handling divisions between congregations and organizations of believers? And if not, why not? Are there means for handling sin, slander and other gross sins in the Body? In the charismatic world, is there justice today? Scripture says that these things were written for our example.

Justice: The Heart Cry of the Prophets

In the faith of ancient Israel, right belief, worship and behavior were inseparable. Most believers are aware that the prophets spoke with great passion when rebuking Israel for turning away from God to serve false gods. Serving the wrong gods led to additional behavior contrary to the Law of God. Conversely, breaking the Law of God made people more disposed to serve false gods. However, justice was at least an equal concern of the prophets.

In ancient Israel, *might was not to make right*. The worship of the one true God was to give an individual the faith and motivation to act with compassion and justice. These two concepts, compassion and justice, are not at all opposed in the prophets. It should be noted therefore that the prophets of God spoke with equal passion against the violation of the principles of justice and idolatry. This heart cry is found throughout the prophets; it ought not be missed. The judges are to be fair and objective, uninfluenced by those who bribe or manipulate politically. Micah sums up the view of the prophets in the following famous words:

> *He has shown you, O man, what is good; and what does the* LORD *require of you but to do justly, to love mercy, and to walk humbly with your God?*
>
> Micah 6:8

This verse comes in the form of a scathing indictment. Micah was giving a bad report! (Yes, brethren, when due process is denied and all attempts at due process have been made, there is a place for a prophetic bad report!) We are told that the leaders stripped the skin from their people (Mic. 3:2). Indeed, God speaks as follows:

> *Shall I count pure those with the wicked balances, and with the bag of deceitful weights? ...her inhabitants have spoken lies....*
>
> Micah 6:11, 12

In Amos we read that Israel sold the righteous for silver and the poor for a pair of sandals (2:6). However, the corruption of the court system was a key to sin's flourishing. Most congregations have no court system! What are the implications? We read the following of the court system or the judges of the gates:

> *They hate the one who rebukes in the gate, and they abhor the one who speaks uprightly. Therefore, because you tread down the poor and take grain taxes from him, though you have built houses of hewn stone, yet you shall not dwell in them....*
>
> Amos 5:10-11

> *You afflict the just and take bribes; you divert the poor from justice at the gate. Therefore the prudent keep silent at that time, for it is an evil time.*
>
> Amos 5:12-13

> *Hate evil, love good; establish justice in the gate. It may be that the LORD God of hosts will be gracious to the remnant of Joseph.*
>
> Amos 5:15

Although the people of God are laughed to scorn, God's promise was and is that His people, if they have a just and compassionate society, would see the nations take positive note and remark about the wisdom in the land. We might ask, could Israel influence the nations for good if she was not a just society? Can the Church salt the society at large if she is not a just society? However, if there is no structure of justice or no clear accountability in the Church, how can we be a just society? Satan can easily send wolves in sheep's clothing, and nothing can be done to stop him.

It was easy for the rich to exploit the poor with taxes and slave wages. It was easy to slander, and to cause the miscarriage of justice where the court structure was corrupt. Jeremiah says:

> *For if you thoroughly amend your ways and your doings, if you thoroughly execute judgment between a*

*man and his neighbor, if you do not oppress the
stranger, the fatherless, and the widow, and do not shed
innocent blood in this place, or walk after other gods to
your hurt, then I will cause you to dwell in this place...*
                                            Jeremiah 7:5-7

Jeremiah makes it clear that being religious through
Temple service would have no effect where justice was
lacking! In contrast, the rule of the Messiah is one that
will bring justice in the land.

*...I will raise to David a Branch of righteousness; a
King shall reign and prosper, and **execute judgment
and righteousness** in the earth.*
                                            Jeremiah 23:5

In the writings of the prophet Isaiah, we have the
most passionate plea for God's people to be a society of
justice. Isaiah constantly provides us with a contrast between Israel with her injustice, lack of standards and unholiness and the just society that the Messiah will bring.
Let us remember that we are the Body of the Messiah.
We are to reflect His ways and bring His will into
manifestation among His people.

The Messiah is a judge; we read of His supernatural
discernment.

*...He shall not judge by the sight of His eyes, nor decide
by the hearing of His ears; but with righteousness He
shall judge the poor, and decide with equity for the meek
of the earth....*
                                            Isaiah 11:3-4

Believers are poorly taught; many do not realize that
this passage is speaking of the Messiah as King-Judge in
the sense that He renders just decisions where issues and
conflicts arise among human beings. Is He only to do
this directly, or also through His Body, His people?

The prophets greatly valued the judicial function. It was a central issue for them that people be trained in character and wisdom for judicial functioning. That is far from today's understanding. Although we bring the lost to Jesus, we fail to prepare a just, corporate body where these new believers can properly mature. In contrast, Isaiah writes these words of the Messiah:

> *A bruised reed He will not break, and smoking flax He will not quench; He will bring forth justice for truth. He will not fail nor be discouraged, till He has established justice in the earth; and the coastlands shall wait for His law.*
>
> Isaiah 42:3-4

Due process and the courts of justice are meant to protect the righteous against the crimes and onslaughts of the wicked. The Law is the key to the meaning of justice. Do we not have many wolves in sheep's clothing in leadership and in the ranks of the Body of the Messiah who slander, extort, commit adultery and abuse the sheep? Yet where is there any means to deal with these people? Are we merely to pray until God zaps them? That will indeed eventually happen, but it is hardly merciful to them. A process of justice might bring them to their senses and to repentance. In the Hebrew Scriptures the meaning of rulership is connected to the dispensing of justice!

Isaiah's Great Justice Chapter

Isaiah's most passionate chapter on justice, in my view, is the magnificent fifty-ninth. The opening verses show that Israel was calling upon God for national deliverance. However, their sins had separated them from God and His deliverance. God, therefore, had hidden His face from them. What were these sins? We read:

For your hands are defiled with blood, and your fingers with iniquity; your lips have spoken lies, your tongue has muttered perversity. (v. 3)

Then, contrary to much Christian teaching that encourages believers to be silent and passive in the face of injustice (e.g., don't take up an offense for another; be loving to all sides in disputes; don't take sides; etc.), Isaiah says:

No one calls for justice, nor does any plead for truth. They trust in empty words and speak lies; they conceive evil and bring forth iniquity. (v. 4)

In other words, God's people are to stand up against injustice! Our lack of teaching on this subject may be the reason why we seem so apathetic about the great issues in our land today. We are not to take a stand outside of biblical principles and processes. We are not to take up offenses in the sense of being bitter and vengeful for the sake of another. However, when the principles of justice are trampled, love demands that we stand for justice. That is the clear lesson from those who stood with the Jewish people in the Holocaust and from those who gave lame excuses not to do so.

Then Isaiah describes the plotting of the wicked, the deceit on their lips and their distance from justice. The lack of justice produces a terrible condition, as described in these words:

Therefore justice is far from us, nor does righteousness overtake us; we look for light, but there is darkness! For brightness, but we walk in blackness! We grope for the wall like the blind, and we grope as if we had no eyes; we stumble at noonday as at twilight; we are as dead men in desolate places. We all growl like bears, and moan sadly like doves; we look for justice, but there is

none; for salvation, but it is far from us. For our trans-
gressions are multiplied before You, and our sins testify
against us; for our transgressions are with us, and as
for our iniquities, we know them: in transgressing and
lying against the LORD, and departing from our God,
speaking oppression and revolt, conceiving and utter-
ing from the heart words of falsehood. (vv. 9-13)

Then come these ringing words:

Justice is turned back, and righteousness stands afar
off; for truth is fallen in the street, and equity cannot
enter. So truth fails, and he who departs from evil
makes himself a prey. (vv. 14-15)

These are judicial words. False testimony causes truth
to fall in the street. Equity cannot enter, for equity is
balanced and sound judgment is based on biblical wisdom. In a circumstance like that, the righteous are persecuted; "he who departs from evil makes himself a
prey."

Again God makes it clear that He expects His people
and leaders to stand for justice, to stand against gross injustice and to depart from those who practice such.
Isaiah says:

...Then the LORD saw it, and it displeased Him that
there was no justice. He saw that there was no man, and
wondered that there was no intercessor.... (vv. 15-16)

Verse 16 is usually applied to intercessory prayer: that
we would pray for the spirit of revival, mercy and forgiveness for our land. That is a true, but secondary, application of the verse. If we have a heart for people, of course
we want them to repent and to know God. We want to
see His deliverance on this basis, not His judgment.

However, our religious tradition has blinded us to the
primary meaning. God was amazed that there was no

one to stand in the gap and call out for justice for those who were denied it! An intercessor is one who stands alongside the one who is denied justice and cries out for it. On this basis, those who stood with the Jewish people during the Holocaust were intercessors. Sometimes an intercessor goes to death or receives persecution when standing with the oppressed. The denial of due process and justice under the law is oppression!

Therefore, what will God do? He will bring justice indeed, but His judgment will be severe! If human instruments under God do not do justice, a more severe judgment will fall upon the land.

> ...Therefore His own arm brought salvation for Him; and His own righteousness, it sustained Him. For He put on righteousness as a breastplate, and a helmet of salvation on His head; He put on the garments of vengeance for clothing, and was clad with zeal as a cloak. According to their deeds, accordingly He will repay, fury to His adversaries, recompense to His enemies; the coastlands He will fully repay. (vv.16-18)

It is a biblical principle: Unjust societies will eventually perish with severe judgment. What does this suggest for unjust congregations and movements that claim the Name of Jesus?

Clearly, when the means of due process and justice are denied, it is the responsibility of the believer to separate from injustice and stand as an intercessor with those who are grossly and unjustly treated. I believe that doing so would greatly change the whole nature of today's church and would be a great beginning toward holiness. The Bible makes it clear that cases of gross sin and error are to be brought before those who sit as judges. The understanding of this principle and its application would greatly diminish the ability of evil leaders to destroy and of immoral people to find a home in the Body of the Messiah!

Justice in the Psalms

The Book of Psalms is filled with expressions that call for the establishment of justice. For some, the call for justice in these psalms is part of a sub-Christian Old Testament perspective. These psalms almost are cleansed of their import for these people, (similar to unbelieving scholars removing the miraculous in their interpretations of the Bible).

It is true that the Psalmist did not have our full perspective on spiritual warfare; he did not have the Name of Jesus and the power of the blood of the Lamb to defeat the forces of the enemy. Yet what of his heart to establish justice? Was it an accurate and trustworthy orientation? Believers have wrestled with the psalms that call for vengeance upon human enemies. So several comments are in order here.

I believe it is true that most of the calls for vengeance on enemies are to be applied to the demonic hosts that war against us. As Paul aptly taught, we wrestle not against flesh and blood, but principalities and powers in the heavenlies (II Cor. 10:4). However, is it not possible by the Spirit of God to also pronounce judgment upon man? Satan works through some kind of invitation from man. Yes, our attitude toward people in general is to be one of love and compassion, whereby we seek their redemption. However, is it not possible for a person to become so wicked that, after a certain point, a proper attitude is to pray that God's judgment may fall upon them? That certainly seems to be the case with the saints in the Book of *Revelation* toward the Antichrist and his leaders.

Secondly, I believe that the emphasis in the Book of Psalms on the king of Israel and the Messiah bringing justice to society has significant implications for leaders in the church now. Although this theme is pervasive in the Book of Psalms, it is truly amazing how little attention it receives. It is almost as if only those passages that are for comfort or are predictive of the Messiah's coming have any relevance!

To be in accord with God, who hates wickedness, must certainly be proper. To preach an easy forgiveness (although we all must remove personal vengeance from our hearts), where in our forgiving others there is no stand to call them to repent of gross sin, is wrong. The words of Psalm 5 are noteworthy.

> *For You are not a God who takes pleasure in wickedness, nor shall evil dwell with You. The boastful shall not stand in Your sight; You hate all workers of iniquity. You shall destroy those who speak falsehood; the* LORD *abhors the bloodthirsty and deceitful man.... For there is no faithfulness in their mouth; their inward part is destruction; their throat is an open tomb; they flatter with their tongue. Pronounce them guilty, O God! Let them fall by their own counsels; cast them out in the multitude of their transgressions, for they have rebelled against You.* (vv. 4-6; 9-10)

The pleas in Psalm 7:9-11 are powerful indeed.

> *Oh, let the wickedness of the wicked come to an end, but establish the just; for the righteous God tests the hearts and minds. My defense is of God, who saves the upright in heart. God is a just judge, and God is angry with the wicked every day.*

The character of God and of the Messiah in administering justice is clear in Psalm 9:8.

He shall judge the world in righteousness, and He shall administer judgment for the peoples in uprightness.

Another call for justice in the face of man's treachery is powerfully brought forth in Psalm 12.

Help, LORD, for the godly man ceases! For the faithful disappear from among the sons of men. They speak idly everyone with his neighbor; with flattering lips and a double heart they speak. May the LORD cut off all flattering lips, and the tongue that speaks proud things. (vv. 1-3)

This cry for vindication for the just and punishment for the wicked and the unrepentant is consistently part of the fabric of the Psalms.

Psalm 37 is one of the most magnificent psalms that deal with the theme of wickedness. The justice of God is again in view.

Depart from evil, and do good; and dwell forevermore. For the LORD loves justice, and does not forsake His saints.... The mouth of the righteous speaks wisdom, and his tongue talks of justice. The law of his God is in his heart; none of his steps shall slide. (vv. 27-28; 30-31)

Since God is the righteous Judge, a people of godly character will seek to establish justice in the midst of the earth. Intense desire for God to judge the wicked is pervasive in Psalms 58 and 59. God assures the Psalmist that with the proper timing, He will fully bring judgment and justice (Ps. 75). His judgment will deliver the oppressed, who are under the burden of unjust authorities (Ps. 76).

Psalm 82 is a stirring call for the judges or leaders in Israel to act with true justice in their courts. God is the Judge of the judges. We read:

God stands in the congregation of the mighty; He judges among the gods [judges]. *How long will you judge unjustly, and show partiality to the wicked? Selah. Defend the poor and fatherless; do justice to the afflicted and needy. Deliver the poor and needy; free them from the hand of the wicked.* (vv. 1-4)

Psalm 84 is another stirring call for God to judge the proud and rebellious. We gain new insight into Psalm 119 if we read it as a guide not only for the individual, but also for leaders and judges among the people of God.

Psalm 141 calls upon God for safety from wicked schemes. However, it indicates that the reason schemes can be effective is that there are wicked leaders or judges. When righteous and just judges reign over the people of God, wickedness cannot be established. Thus we read, "Their judges are overthrown by the sides of the cliff" (v. 6a).

The wisdom of the Book of Proverbs give a full account of the differences between the wicked and the righteous in many areas of life. The Law of God provides the source of wisdom for rendering fair judgment.

It is amazing to see how far the Body of the Messiah has departed from these sentiments! Have we not created our own interpretive grid or approach to the Bible, in which this major emphasis of the Hebrew Scriptures is hardly a part of our emphasis? Of course, the reader will often hear that these teachings are from the Old Testament and that the New Testament presents a different ideal. But does it? Our next chapter shall address this question.

CHAPTER III

THE JUSTICE OF GOD IN THE NEW TESTAMENT

The words of the prophet Jeremiah are true for many segments of the American Church today.

Run to and fro through the streets of Jerusalem; see now and know; and seek in her open places if you can find a man, if there is anyone who executes judgment, who seeks the truth, and I will pardon her.

Jeremiah 5:1

Many in the Body of believers do not believe that today's church is to be a just society, with the processes and structure to secure justice. Love has been viewed as the opposite of justice rather than as the motive to seek justice. Some think that justice is a proper concern of our society at large, and even that the church is to seek to influence society to justice. However, that the church itself is to be a just society is a wholly new thought for many!

The Background of New Testament Teaching

The New Testament assumes the teaching of the Hebrew Scriptures as the background for its true understanding. However, the structure for obtaining justice in

New Testament days was quite different than in the days of Israel's kings. One important difference was that Israel did not have her independence, but was kept by force within the commonwealth of the Roman Empire. The ultimate jurisdiction for many justice issues was the Roman court. That especially included cases where the penalty was capital punishment. However, Jewish courts still functioned within the land of Israel. The Romans were fully willing to allow these courts to handle many types of cases. Just where the jurisdiction of the Jewish courts ended and where Roman courts were mandated is a matter of some debate. It is especially debated with regard to the stoning of Stephen, the trials of Paul and specifically in the crucifixion of Jesus.

It is plain that at the time of Jesus, the highest Jewish court of appeal was the Sanhedrin. We do not read of such a body in the Hebrew Scriptures. In the Hebrew Scriptures, the high priest had a major judicial role. The Sanhedrin was made up of leading elders from different religious parties in Judaism (Sadducees and Pharisees). The Sanhedrin, as the supreme court, could decide to hear a case or to not receive an appeal. If they decided not to hear an appeal, the decision of the lower court would hold.

What, however, were the lower courts? It would appear that, in the inter-testamental period, the institution of the elders of the gate was replaced by the elders of the synagogue. Therefore, the synagogue functioned in judicial matters, especially on religious questions. More serious questions still could be heard by leading elders of a city. That the synagogue was ruled by men who were called elders clearly indicates their judicial function.

Despite all of the debate concerning which religious party Jesus was the closest to (Pharisees, Sadducees, Essenes and Zealots), it is clear to me that Jesus was closest to the viewpoint of the Pharisees. Hence, in Matthew 23, Jesus taught that the scribes and Pharisees sit in Moses' seat. People were to follow their decisions. Jesus was not teaching that His disciples had to believe in all manner of pharisaic doctrine and religious practice. His example is clearly at variance with that idea. Rather, He recognized that their legitimate function was to serve as the judges in the courts throughout most of the land of Israel. They performed the function of judgment that was carried out by the elders of Israel whom Moses had. appointed. Citizenship in Israel required following the law of the land and the decisions of the courts where such was not contrary to the revealed Word of God. I believe that by this time, the courts of Israel were mostly in the hands of the Pharisees. However, the high court was composed of mostly Sadducees, with pharisaic representatives. In ancient Israel, appeal went from judges who were not Levites, to the high court which was Levitical!

The Parallel for the New Testament Church

Jesus' instruction is similar to how we would instruct believers today to be good citizens in whatever land they reside. It includes obeying the laws of the land and the decisions of the courts where they are not contrary to Scripture. Paul enjoins the same for Christians in the Roman structure (Rom. 13). One must disobey where the law is against Scripture.

Jesus Establishes a New Society

However, from Matthew 16 it becomes clear that Yeshua is forming His own society or congregation (*kahilah*). *Kahilah* is a term that can refer to a synagogue. This congregation (which will be made up of many congregations) is to be built upon the confession of the fact that Yeshua is Messiah and Lord. This society will be a righteous remnant in the midst of Israel and eventually in all of the nations of the world.

The announcement of the Kingdom of God in Jesus' preaching prepares us for this society. The Kingdom of God theme, as expressed in the prophets, looked forward to an ideal age in which the nations will come to the knowledge of God and peace and prosperity will be fully manifested. Jesus' announcement brought a new stage of the Kingdom of God where the realities of the age to come broke into this age. The Kingdom came in Jesus, but it has not yet come in fullness. One key manifestation of the Kingdom of God will be that God's Law and justice will be established in the earth. So in this stage of partial fulfillment of the promise of the Kingdom, in this transitional age, the manifestation of justice and righteousness is to be the society that Jesus established on the basis of Peter's confession, "You are the Messiah, the Son of the living God" (see Matthew 16:16).

This gives us a key for understanding the relationship between the Hebrew Scriptures and the New Testament. The Hebrew Scriptures present us with a limited manifestation of the Kingdom of God. In the Hebrew Scriptures the power of the Holy Spirit was not available to all. Furthermore, the hope of the prophets, that all nations would come to the knowledge of God, was rarely demonstrated. In the New Covenant, the Kingdom is extended to the nations, and Jew and Gentile come under the rule of Jesus. It is a stage of Kingdom manifestation that looks forward to the coming of the Kingdom in fullness, even the Age to Come.

The Kingdom in this transitional age is seen in the life of believing families, in the lives of individuals, in all the areas of life they touch and especially in the life of the Church. The Church, or congregation of Yeshua, does not wield the sword, and her courts do not have the power of corporal punishments or imprisonments. However, the Body of believers is to be a just society that can require repentance, reconciliation, restitution and restoration, or ultimately disfellowshipping, as its means of maintaining itself as a just society.

The chapters of Matthew 16, 18 and 21 provide us with clear teaching on the nature of this new society, the way it is to be governed, the principles of due process by which justice will be established in it and the fact that the rule of the elders of this society is to take precedence over both the Sanhedrin and the elders in Israel who do not follow Yeshua the Messiah.

The Meaning of Binding and Loosing (Matt. 16, 18)

Matthew 16:16 records Peter's great confession of Jesus as the Messiah, the Son of God. This confession is the basis, or foundation, of the congregation that Jesus will build. Jesus then goes on to say:

> ...I will build My church, and the gates of Hades shall not prevail against it. And I will give you the keys to the kingdom of heaven, and whatever you bind on earth will be bound in heaven, and whatever you loose on earth will be loosed in heaven. (vv. 18-19)

Many have taken this passage as a foundation for our authority in prayer, and rightly so. However, I do not believe that that is the primary meaning of the passage. The keys of the Kingdom had a specific meaning within Judaism at the time, as reflected in the Talmud. The keys were understood to be the delegated authority for judicial decisions in Israel, the covenant nation. The members of the Sanhedrin, as the highest court in Israel, understood themselves to possess the keys to the Kingdom of Heaven. The keys were understood to include the right to permit some activities and to forbid other activities. To bind is to forbid, to loose is to permit. After the fall of Jerusalem and the disbanding of the Sanhedrin, the leading rabbis understood themselves to have this authority. This situation is reflected in the Talmud as well. (The Talmud is a compendium of Jewish law, debate, story and legend. It was put into a written format from the third to the sixth centuries.)

Chapters 16, 18 and 21 of Matthew record the incidents whereby our Lord transferred spiritual authority from the Sanhedrin to the apostles. Matters governing the behavior of believers were ultimately in the hands of the apostles. Jesus did leave realms of civil authority in the hands of both the Pharisees and the Roman authorities. However, the higher authority of the apostles included the areas of correct biblical doctrine and behavior. Following the dictates of either the rabbis or the Roman authorities had to be within the boundaries of gospel standards. Hence Peter's famous response to the illegitimate exercise of authority: "We ought to obey God rather than men" (Acts 5:29).

Matthew 16 establishes this new authority of the apostles through Peter as representative and head of the apostolic band. Matthew 18 provides us with another installment in the process of transferring authority. Verse 15 begins by noting the proper procedure for dealing with a brother who has sinned. The one who is sinned against is to go to that brother and seek to restore him, thus gaining him back. If the brother who sinned will not hear, the other is to bring two or three brothers to stand as witnesses to the confrontation. The passage in Matthew quotes from Deuteronomy 17:6: "By the mouth of

two or three witnesses every word may be established"
(Matt. 18:16).

This quote immediately places us in a context where
judges render a decision. A decision of guilt should be
based on the clear and solid foundation of credible witnesses. These witnesses are to urge the brother to
repent. Following such a procedure shows us that the sin
is serious. If the brother repents at this stage, no judicial
action is necessary. We note, however, that certain kinds
of sins disqualify persons from leadership positions in
the Body of the Messiah, at least for a time. In these
cases, there is still a need to bring out the truth so that
the brother will step down from leadership for restoration, even if sin is acknowledged and a profession of
turning from it is made.

If there is no success at the second stage, the witnesses tell the congregation through the leadership.
That gives the congregation an opportunity to plead with
the brother or sister, that a response of repentance might
come about. However, if even the congregation cannot
win him or her to repentance, then we read, "Let him be
to you like a heathen and a tax collector" (Matt. 18:17).
This pronouncement implies several thoughts. First, it
would be the elders of the congregation who sit in judgment, who would make the final pronouncement. That
was the case of the elders at the gate in ancient times, the
elders of the synagogue and by implication the elders of
the congregation of Jesus. The twelve disciples of Jesus
are viewed as having ultimate eldership over the Church.
The original band of apostles is the ultimate eldership
authority for all believers through the New Testament
Scriptures. Paul and the other apostles later appointed
other elders who would serve as authorities in various
congregations throughout the world. These leaders also

would be called upon to exercise an authority according to what is written here.

The penalty enjoined in Matthew is that the person under discipline be viewed as an unbeliever, a heathen and a tax collector. These are people in need of redemption! If a person cannot repent of significant sin and be reconciled to brothers and sisters, we are not to accept them as members of the congregation. Only God knows the heart, but our response should follow the evidence.

I believe that the judicial procedures of those times made it clear that the elders were to bring forth the final judgment, after all the steps have been taken, and to say, "With regard to the gospel, John Doe is now to be considered among us as an unbeliever, and one who is even especially in need of redemption."

In the epistles we are given further instruction on how to respond to such a person, that the Name of Jesus not be dishonored.

In this context Jesus again says:

> *Assuredly, I say to you, whatever you bind on earth will be bound in heaven, and whatever you loose on earth will be loosed in heaven. Again I say to you that if two of you agree on earth concerning anything that they ask, it will be done for them by My Father in heaven. For where two or three are gathered together in My name, I am there in the midst of them.*
>
> Matthew 18:18-20

The decision of disfellowshipping enjoined in this passage is connected to the judicial function of binding and loosing. It is one type of binding and loosing. There are others. In Acts 15 the Gentiles were loosed from the requirement of being Jews. Disfellowshipping binds the individual from calling himself a believer in the midst of God's congregation. It also binds us to not have fellowship with him as if he were a brother. That is a clear implication of his being as a heathen or tax collector. This concept is also made explicit in the epistles of Paul.

Two or three judges in the Name of Jesus can make such a decision. Jesus is in the midst of such a court and backs the decisions done in His Name and will. Even so, the Talmud makes it clear that three judges form a proper judicial court (a *Bet Din*). This passage also contains implications for prayer in the "will of God." However, the context is in asking God to back the judicial decisions of the leadership of the congregation of Yeshua.

Kingdom Authority Has Been Transferred

The parable in Matthew 21:33-46 (which is found in the other synoptic Gospels as well) brings out the truth that the authority of the Kingdom of God on earth has been transferred to the apostles. This truth is also implied in Matthew 16 and 18. However, the authority transfer is explicit in this passage.

The parable of the landowner is one of the few allegories in the New Testament. We are presented with a landowner who put his vineyard under a group of vinedresser stewards. When the landowner sought to collect the fruit of the vineyard, the vinedresser stewards beat his servants and killed one. Other servants were sent and treated the same way. Finally the son of the landowner was sent, but they even killed the son. A question is then asked: What will the owner of the vineyard do to these unfaithful stewards when he comes? The points of reference are clear. Israel, the people of God, is the vineyard of God. The religious leaders are the stewards. They have a historic heritage of mistreating and even killing the prophets of God. Finally, they seek to destroy the Son of the Owner of the vineyard. The Son of God the Father is Jesus.

The people rightly answer the question, that the owner will destroy those wicked men and give his vineyard to other vinedressers. For our purposes, verse 43 is important. Jesus said:

Therefore I say to you, the kingdom of God will be taken from you and given to a nation bearing the fruits of it.

This verse is sometimes wrongly understood to be a prophecy of the Church replacing Israel. However, the vineyard is Israel and all who are grafted into the olive tree. It is not a replacement of Israel that is in view, but a replacement of the ruling elite. The word "nation" in Greek can have broad meanings, referring to a tribe or societal group as well as to a concept related more to our modern nation-states. Obviously Jesus is speaking here of an authority transfer. We read:

Now when the chief priests and Pharisees heard His parables, they perceived that He was speaking of them. But when they sought to lay hands on Him, they feared the multitudes, because they took Him for a prophet. (vv. 45-46).

This transfer of authority is from the chief priests and Pharisees to the apostles. The people did not hear Jesus teaching a replacement of Israel, but of leadership. It is more clear in the verson of Luke 20, where the words are, "He will come and destroy those vinedressers and give the vineyard to others" (v. 16).

The Apostles Demonstrate Their Authority to Bind and Loose

In Acts 15 we see the effect of the transfer of authority as the apostles and elders at Jerusalem exercise the authority to bind and loose. The issue here is the prerequisites for fellowship to be placed upon Gentiles. The decision in Acts 15 does not loose Jews from Jewish calling. It does, however, loose Gentiles from the requirements of Jewish calling. They are still bound with regard to not eating blood (a standard that began with Noah, which includes not eating what is strangled), and abstaining from meat offered to idols and from immorality (which implies all of God's basic ethical standards of right and wrong). The Jerusalem council acts as the high court for all believers in this major decision.

On the other hand, we see no Roman-type hierarchy established by the apostles. Apparently they believed that able leaders could be called together again if necessary. The present divisions in the church today make doing that difficult. The result of the transfer of authority is also seen in the fact that ordinary decisions of discipline are vested in local elderships, with the input of apostolic leadership.

The Appointing of Elders

The original apostles appointed elders to carry on the functions of teaching the Word, of ordering the congregation in spreading the gospel and in maintaining discipline in the life of the congregation. The Book of Acts shows Paul leaving his congregations in the hands of a plurality of elders in city after city (Acts 14:23). They were given the authority to rule and by implication to judge and to bind and loose.

Timothy was given the authority under Paul to appoint elders. The instructions given to him are crucial in understanding the role of elders and the standards for choosing them. Titus was given similar instructions in the letter written to him (chapter 1). We shall emphasize the instructions in First Timothy 3. I believe the terms "elder" and "bishop" (overseer) describe the same function. However, this book was not written to settle the question of God's type of government structure. Most of what we say can be applied to different structures of government. (The booklet, *Models of Accountability*, addresses this question of government structure.)

Standards for Elders

I believe that First Timothy 3:1-13 is one of the most "rationalized away" chapters in the Bible. The standards of this chapter are not impossible to meet. Yet the extent to which these standards are not enforced in the Church today is a little short of amazing.

To desire to be an overseer is a good thing if the motive is to more fully serve the Kingdom of God. Love should be the basis of desiring to see an increase in our usefulness in the Kingdom.

An overseer must be the husband of one wife. I believe this standard probably implies that a divorce and remarriage after coming to know Jesus is not an option for one in leadership. It disqualifies one from leadership. It certainly means that anyone who has been divorced and remarried while claiming to be a believer, and who was without biblical grounds for divorce and remarriage, cannot be an overseer in the Body of believers. On this point alone we see an extraordinary departure from historic standards in the American Church today. If the personality is charismatic (which we often dub as anointed!), the backslidden leader needs only to bide his time until being accepted again as a leader by a large segment of the Body. Many will say, "Who are we to judge?" That makes a mockery of the standards apostolically enjoined.

Beyond his marriage, we read a list of other character traits required for one to be recognized as an elder:

> *...temperate, sober-minded, of good behavior, hospitable, able to teach; not given to wine, not violent, not greedy for money, but gentle, not quarrelsome, not covetous ... not a novice, lest being puffed up with pride he fall into the same condemnation as the devil. Moreover he must have a good testimony among those who are outside, lest he fall into reproach and the snare of the devil.*
>
> I Timothy 3:2-3, 6-7

The next standard is extremely important. We read:

> *...one who rules his own house well, having his children in submission with all reverence (for if a man does not know how to rule his own house, how will he take care of the church of God?).*
>
> I Timothy 3:4-5

This verse clearly shows that successful family headship is the key prerequisite for eldership. Elder rule is given to men who have proven their ability in family life. There may be exceptions to the rule, but that is the rule! In addition, I believe that gift ministers of Ephesians 4 (apostles, prophets, evangelists, pastors and teachers) are called to fulfill eldership, or at least deacon standards.

Family headship is the proving ground because of what must be proven. In the family, a man proves his ability to discipline, to give delegated authority to his wife and to act as judicial authority in the home. If he does these things well, he will have a well-ruled family. His judicial function will be put to the test intensely in handling disputes among his children. Children look to the parents and ultimately to the father for fair judgment in times of strife. The parents must teach the principles of love, repentance, forgiveness and restitution through family experiences. The family thus becomes a peaceable kingdom.

Successful biblical rulership in the family, with the rest of the prerequisites fulfilled, is the full and adequate preparation for recognizing eldership. If believers would demand that elders have a good marriage and a rightly ordered family life, the quality of godliness in the Body of the Messiah would improve greatly.

Eldership and Judicial Functioning

The designations of "elder" and "overseer" assume the judicial functions of the leaders of the congregations since the background of their use is the synagogue and its rulers. To the elders is given the responsibility of ensuring that discipling takes place in a context where the gospel is being spread. True conversions provide a people willing to be discipled! In this context, the elders are to enforce the basic standards of the Word for membership and the more rigorous standards for leaders.

In order to enforce these standards, the elders must be able to see that the standards of due process in Matthew 18 are followed. In addition, no leader is to ever be part of a structure of government where he is not truly accountable and thus subject to biblical discipline. What could be more apparent than the fact that when a leader sins in a way where he no longer fulfills the standards of First Timothy 3, he needs to step down or be removed? How far today's practice is from these standards! In an "anything goes" manner, many establish themselves as leaders simply by hanging up a shingle. There is no endorsement from other leaders or testimony that these people fulfill biblical standards! New Testament leaders were not self-appointed. Many today set up structures where they cannot be removed if they fall into sin!

Under a misapplication of the word "forgiveness," we allow many people to continue in leadership ministries who do not fulfill biblical standards! How can we influence society toward righteousness when such righteousness is seriously lacking in the Body of believers?

The Commandment to Establish Courts

First Corinthians 5 and 6 are very important chapters in clarifying the judicial function of elders. In these chapters we are given an example of how to apply standards of righteousness in a situation of gross sin. We also are provided with a list of capital offenses that require disfellowshipping, as well as a description of what that entails. In addition, there is an injunction to establish a court to settle disputes between believers. If there is true repentance, Second Corinthians makes it clear that the erring brother is to be fully received back.

In First Corinthians 5:1-9 we are told of a man in the fellowship who was in an incestuous relationship with his father's wife (probably a stepmother). That relationship is clearly forbidden in Leviticus 18. This issue, by the way, shows Paul's affirmation of the moral standards of the Torah for all his congregations. Paul, as an apostle, notes his judicial authority in this case in verse 3. The congregation is to gather together in the power of the Name of Jesus to officially disfellowship this person and to...

> *...deliver such a one to Satan for the destruction of the flesh, that his spirit may be saved in the day of the Lord Jesus.* (v. 5)

Paul's instruction is in line with Matthew 18, where Jesus puts the one who sinned in the midst of his judges

when the decision of disfellowshipping is made. Furthermore, the decision to disfellowship binds all congregants
from fellowshipping with the person who professes to be
a believer but who lives in gross sin. The purpose of this
severe discipline is to shock the person into sensibility
and repentance. It also protects the flock against falsely
professing people, or wolves. There is protection in the
covering of the Body of Believers. Satan might then seek
to destroy the flesh with sickness. Yet even that could
lead to repentance instead of to both spiritual and physi-
cal destruction.

If a person calls himself a believer but continues in
gross sin, he undercuts the honor of the Name of Jesus.
Every believer is an ambassador in His Name. The Name
of God is holy; all who name His Name as believers are
to reflect that holiness. If the prophet proclaimed that
God's name was profaned among the Gentiles because
of Israel, how much more does the rebuke apply to the
Church!

The specific instructions given here by Paul lead to
general instructions concerning the nature of discipline.
We are told that the Body is to purge out the old leaven,
a symbol of corruption and evil. The leaven of malice
and wickedness must not be allowed to remain in the fellowship of the saints. Evil reports and slander destroy
trust and the unity of community.

That does not mean we are not to have any contact
with unbelievers. How then would the gospel be spread?
The issue is the honor of the Name of Jesus and the
purity of the fellowship of the saints. Discipline is enjoined in situations of gross deception, where a person
claims to be a believer while living in gross sin. *It is a
clear principle of the gospel. It is totally unnecessary for any
truly born again believer to live in gross sin. No excuse for im-
maturity or process of growth is allowed where gross sin is concerned. Any true conversion is an immediate turning from*

gross sin. Paul makes this principle explicit in the following teaching:

> *I wrote to you in my epistle not to keep company with sexually immoral people. Yet I certainly did not mean with the sexually immoral people of this world, or with the covetous, or extortioners, or idolaters, since then you would need to go out of the world. But now I have written to you not to keep company with anyone named a brother, who is a fornicator, or covetous, or an idolater, or a reviler, or a drunkard, or an extortioner—not even to eat with such a person. For what have I to do with judging those also who are outside? Do you not judge those who are inside? But those who are outside God judges. Therefore, "put away from yourselves that wicked person."*

I Corinthians 5:9-13

The last verse is a quote from Deuterononmy 13. God requires a basic purity to be maintained in His covenant community. Paul's teaching here is foundational. Against all of the "sloppy agape" in today's church, which says we are not to judge (a misunderstanding of the command in Matthew not to have a condemning attitude), Paul commands us to judge those inside. We can relate to all kinds of sinners in outreach. However, only those whose lives manifest basic, biblical moral standards may be accepted as members of the fellowship of the saints.

Disfellowshipping is the ultimate judicial sanction in the Body of the Messiah. The Body is not to be a civil government exacting a death penalty. However, the list of gross sins that require disfellowshipping parallel the sins in the Torah that required death or exile from Israel. That we are not to eat with such a person reflects the fact that eating together in the Jewish world has the connotation of brotherly acceptance.

We must ask several questions from this passage. First, does today's church world follow these instructions? The answer in many quarters is definitely not! Are Christians trained to maintain legitimately enjoined discipline and to avoid those who are disfellowshipped? A humanistic mercy often leads believers to reject the claims of discipline, to the great injury of not only the person under discipline, but also the Body of the Messiah. When standards of discipline are followed, the maximum potential for repentance and salvation is released. *It is a clear standard of the New Testament; that which required capital punishment in the Hebrew Scriptures requires disfellowshipping in the New Testament.*

Gross doctrinal error is presented as another grounds for disfellowshipping. It is clear from Deuteronomy 13 where the people are warned against the false prophet who would call them to follow other gods. It is also plain in Galatians 1, which concerns any person who would preach another gospel. Such a person is to be placed under a curse or, by obvious implication, disfellowshipped.

Does Today's Church Follow These Instructions?

One of the strange facts of our contemporary church life is that persons in gross sin and doctrinal error are not disciplined. Leaders who become disqualified, according to standards in First Timothy 3, are not removed. Yet those who are not in gross doctrinal and moral error, according to biblical standards, are slandered and shunned for holding to differing doctrinal interpretations on nonessential matters. Many are terribly slandered and shunned without the due process of Matthew 18.

Church leaders are soft on extreme sin and error while other leaders are harsh and critical where there is no serious sin and error at all. Many times the person who is accused does not even believe the view of which he is accused. Perhaps he used a phrase or a biblical term that was associated with a false interpretation in the mind of the critic. Without any due process, the person is blasted from the housetops with slanderous accusations. It is the accuser who is in gross sin; for slander and character assasination is a sin that is to be punished by disfellowshipping! May God help us. An adulterer is received while he calls upon believers to separate from others, on the grounds that their views on the timing of the rapture and the Great Tribulation are wrong! Such a scenario is not hypothetical; it has really happened. Amazingly, many follow his call!

Another fact of contemporary church life concerns those who seek to follow these Scriptures. It is obvious that if one congregation legitimately disciplines, with due process, its decision should be upheld and followed by other congregations. However, there is competition in the land of the free. Many leaders want more bodies in their congregations, even if growth is through lateral transfer and not from evangelism. Hence the one under discipline usually can find a congregation where the leader will receive his slanders and lies against the congregation that disciplined him. Will this leader seek to talk to the leaders of the other congregations and get the facts? Perhaps he holds to a different theology of the last days. Besides, any group that disciplines must be in the "shepherding error." At least, that is the assumption of the First Church of Anarchy. And yet, the pastor of the First Church of Anarchy will be the first to blast the group that believes in discipline as holding to false doctrine. No due process is deemed necessary before such slander is spread.

If we do not seek to uphold the decisions of congregational elders as the judiciary of the courts of the Church, to uphold discipline in an inter-congregational way, all of the instructions of Jesus and Paul in this area are of no effect.

It is a principle of human behavior that when we do not enforce biblical, moral standards, we fall into furthering our own legalistic standards! (The issue of inter-congregational relations with regard to upholding discipline will be dealt with in Chapter V. The reader already has some sense of my convictions from what has been said here.) The reformers stated that God's ideal was a church that would require unity in essentials, liberty in nonessentials and in all things a motive of love. We have hardly followed this wonderful biblical ideal. What I am laying out may seem new to some; however, it is the historic position of evangelical Protestantism!

Courts to Settle Disputes

In chapter 6 of First Corinthians, we see Paul amazed that believers were going before pagans in the Roman courts to settle their disputes. Yet the saints will be the judiciary in the world to come. It is time for us to prepare by picking from our midst those who are most qualified to judge and mediate disputes.

If we will judge angels, should we not even appoint those who are least esteemed among us to judge disputes, rather than to go to the courts of the world? For believers to fight in the courts of the world discredits the gospel and shows that we are not a community of redeemed and reconciled human beings. It is the opposite of Kingdom manifestation. Elders are given the

function to judge cases that arise. Paul says with great
irony:

> ...*Is it so, that there is not a wise man among you, not
> even one, who will be able to judge between his brethren?*
> I Corinthians 6:5

It is better to be defrauded than to discredit the
gospel. Surely, however, if we have true biblical elders,
they could sit in judgment and weigh the evidence with
the wisdom of the Holy Spirit. In making judgment, we
are to keep in mind that...

> ...*the unrighteous will not inherit the kingdom of
> God...Neither fornicators, nor idolaters, nor adulterers,
> nor homosexuals, nor sodomites, nor thieves, nor
> covetous, nor drunkards, nor revilers, nor extortioners
> will inherit the Kingdom of God.*
> I Corinthians 6:9-10

My primary reason for dealing with these Scriptures
is to present the biblical truth that we are to establish
courts in the Church to discipline gross sin and doctrinal
error and to settle disputes between believers. The eldership courts also remove leaders who become disqualified
and who do not voluntarily step down.

New believers are like children in spiritual maturity.
Thus there will always be a need for this function, to settle disputes. The verse in First Corinthians does not indicate that a believer should not go to court against an
unbeliever. He may need to do so to protect society from
a criminal. But his motive should not be revenge. A disfellowshipped person could be taken to court as an unbeliever in some cases. However, our concern for
furthering the Kingdom must always take precedence
over any concern for personal justice.

The first century church took these passages seriously. By the end of the century, the courts of the Church

were known for their standards of fairness and justice. Voluntarily, unbelievers sought to submit their disputes to the courts of the Church rather than to the corrupt Roman courts.

The Church at the End of the Twentieth Century

If we look at the church of the nineteenth century, we see a church experiencing periodic revivals in a structure that sought to maintain basic standards with biblically derived principles of due process through a form of church courts. It was true of the Puritan movements of the seventeenth and eighteenth centuries. It was true of Methodists, Baptists, Brethren, Lutherans, Presbyterians, Free Church denominations, Holiness denominations and the early Pentecostal denominations that arose in the twentieth century. That does not mean they were perfect in this area. There were times when they fell short. However, there was a general consensus on those issues of discipline.

What has happened? Where are the courts of the Church at the end of the twentieth century? In our apostasized denominations, the courts exist mostly on paper. Because many historic denominations gave up their doctrinal and moral standards between 1900 and 1960, few standards are left to enforce. Other denominations no longer enforce standards like they used to (there are exceptions). Many new Christian movements believe that enforcing standards compromises freedom in the Spirit. The very concept of courts of the Church would seem restrictive and deadening to the leaders of the First Charismatic Church of Anarchy. Thank God for those denominations and movements that are exceptions to this attitude.

We live in a world where anyone can appoint himself a leader. They rationalize that it is God who appoints;

not man. It is true that God appoints. However, it is also important that mature leaders, who fulfill the standards of First Timothy 3, endorse the new leaders as also fulfilling such standards. It is important that every leader be truly accountable and removable by others, according to clearly publicized processes.

A planter of a new work should be *officially* accountable to outside elders. How else can the standards of these chapters and the call for enforcing standards take place? Yes, God Himself will judge. However, to leave judgment only to Him and to not enforce standards according to biblical injunctions is to invite a more severe judgment. That is not mercy, but deception. "Recognize those who labor among you" the Scriptures enjoin (I Thess. 5:12). We know that the apostolic leaders gave letters to accredit those who traveled in ministry. To "recognize those who labor" means that we have at least ascertained their fulfilling of biblical standards for leadership and that they are truly accountable. Such accountability clearly was present in the church at the end of the first century. Real accountability means submission to those who can remove disqualified leaders and who can discipline gross sin and error.

Who Should We Accept in Leadership?

Miracles alone do not attest to the identity of a servant of God. The faith of those who were ministered to can be the reason for the miracle. There are character standards for members and leaders! Because we do not act according to these biblical standards today, Satan has many plants in the midst of the church.

The education of believers in these principles is a pressing necessity. This need is shown when a group disciplines and removes a leader and fans among the Christian public and other movements quickly endorse that fallen leader and make him part of themselves. *"Tell it not in Gath"* the prophet Micah proclaims (1:10). The Name of God is blasphemed among the nations (as was said of ancient Israel) because of us. May God grant us repentance that we might fully seek to follow His Word.

CHAPTER IV

JUSTICE AND MERCY

Then He spoke a parable to them, that men always ought to pray and not lose heart, saying: "There was in a certain city a judge who did not fear God nor regard man. Now there was a widow in that city; and she came to see him, saying, 'Avenge me of my adversary.' And he would not for a while; but afterward he said within himself, 'Though I do not fear God nor regard man, yet because this widow troubles me I will avenge her, lest by her continual coming she weary me.' " Then the Lord said, "Hear what the unjust judge said. And shall God not avenge His own elect who cry out day and night to Him, though He bears long with them? I tell you that He will avenge them speedily. Nevertheless, when the Son of Man comes, will He really find faith on the earth?"

Luke 18:1-8

This remarkable parable makes it clear that God is very concerned for justice. Of course God is not like the unjust judge. He is the Judge of all the earth who will always do right. In His mercy, He delays His justice that people might repent, but His judgment will come eventually. God also will avenge the persecutors of His elect, unless these persecutors repent. The martyrs in Revelation 6 cry out and ask how long it will be until their blood is avenged (v.10).

Sadly, many believers have been indoctrinated into a gospel of indulgence in which concepts such as love, mercy and grace are seen as contrary to justice. Many believers have been taught that a hellfire is for un-believers, but that we who are under the blood of the Lamb have a God completely indulgent toward us so we also must be indulgent to others. To enforce historic standards for members and leaders is seen as overly or-ganizational, unmerciful, unloving, ungracious and even "Old Testamentish"!

Yet as the parable notes, God has not been converted from a vengeful to a merciful God since the days of the Old Testament. God has always been a God of justice, mercy and love!

Relating Love, Justice and Mercy

Because God loves us and is still just, we have a dilem-ma. How can God be accounted just by His own stand-ards, and yet forgive and bless? The answer is in the cross. The full penalty of justice was paid on the cross, and because we are in Him, we are accounted as having paid the price justice demands. To be accounted righteous, we must, by His power, repent of our sins. True repentance always includes restitution wherever it is possible. We do not deserve this grace, yet in mercy God offers it. He can offer it only because the cross satis-fies His standards of justice.

The previous paragraph is a summary of the way of salvation through Jesus, as found in Romans chapters 5 and 6. A truly born again person desires to live righteously and is empowered by the Holy Spirit to turn from gross sin. After turning from such sin there is a lifetime of growth into perfection. Leaders are not perfect, but they have achieved a level of success in sanctification and fruit-bearing that causes others to look to them for discipling.

When a believer sins by lying, stealing, slandering or teaching false doctrine, that believer must repent. If repentance is true, the one who stole returns the stolen goods, plus extra compensation, according to scriptural standards. Because of the cross, and of our sincere repentance and restitution, God does not hold us eternally accountable for our violation. Our sin is under the blood. However, it is not under the blood if there is no repentance. There is no real repentance if there is no restitution. The slanderer must do all in his power to restore the reputation of the individual or of the group slandered. The one who taught false doctrine seeks to inform all who were mistaught of what was false so that any wrong influence is nullified.

This process demonstrates how mercy, love and justice come together in the plan of God. The prophets understood it. If God indulged those who "ripped off" the poor, it would not be merciful, but grossly unloving toward the victims! When Zacchaeus repented, he said, "Look, Lord, I give half of my goods to the poor, and if I have taken anything from anyone by false accusation, I restore it fourfold." Jesus responded, "Today salvation has come to this house, because he also is a son of Abraham." (See Luke 19:1-10.) What if Zacchaeus had said, "Look, Lord, I thank you that you are loving and forgiving and even though I have stolen and been bad, I now receive your love"? I am certain that Jesus would not have responded positively. However, in today's church world, one group could require someone to repent and make restitution while another group could respond that such requirement was harsh and judgmental, that the situation was under the blood. Only sincere repentance puts sin under the blood, and there is no sincere repentance without truly desiring to make restitution.

Yes, God longs for us to receive His mercy, but He cannot provide it in such a way as to violate His justice. He longs to apply the cleansing blood of Jesus, but He can apply it only to the truly repentant. That is the nature of God's mercy, love and justice. It is a love so deep that He sent Jesus to die for us. It is a justice so true that it required the death of Jesus for our sins and our repentance to receive it. Thus God is "just and the Justifier" of those who are in Jesus.

Those who understand God's mercy and love to be indulgence toward those who are in sin cause unrighteousness to prevail in the Body of the Messiah and demean the work of the cross. They have a humanistic concept of mercy, not a biblical one!

When a person truly repents and seeks to make restitution, the offended party may not only forgive so as to restore the relationship, but also forgive the debt for which restitution is to be made. That is a free gift. However, he is not free to forgive the debt for another or to release from restitution if doing so would demean the righteousness of God. At times it is more loving to require restitution, so that moral fiber might be built in the offender. With regard to monetary compensation, each circumstance should be considered. A person who habitually steals may need the discipline of restitution to grow. In cases of gross slander, the fabric of community is torn. To restore trust and love in a community, restitution is almost always necessary. So the offended party should not be required to forego restitution; such a debt cancellation is a free gift.

It is the responsibility of the elders in a local congregation, and of leading figures beyond the local scene in inter-congregational matters, to see that gross sin and error is dealt with and that restitution is made. Biblical standards of due process and evidence must be followed. *Due process is interwoven into the whole context of the Scriptures and is a central part of biblical justice.*

When a Leader Falls into Gross Sin

If a leader falls into gross sin or error, I believe biblical standards require that that leader be removed from leadership and undergo a process of restoration and counseling. Restoration includes public confession and requalifying. To not do so is to lower the standards of the Body of the Messiah. Some sins may possibly disqualify a person from leadership for life. To simply say, "I repent, it's under the blood and God has forgiven; I am continuing in leadership," makes a mockery of biblical standards. Yes, God forgives. However, a truly repentant person is concerned more for the glory of the Name of God. He gladly receives discipline so that God's Name might be honored. The truly repentant will not see their gifts and calling as more important to God than the issue of upholding His standard of holiness and thereby glorifying His Name.

Some have even lamely claimed that their continuing in ministry would help others understand that we serve a forgiving God and that we are sinners saved by grace. We *were* sinners, but we now have the power (the grace) to do right. We have no excuse for falling into gross sin. Indeed, God forgives. That the leader might be restored after requalifying is due to His mercy. God also wants to be merciful to the sheep. He knows that leaders who are allowed to remain in leadership after falling into great sin and error will raise the temptation level for the sheep. "If he can do it and get off so easily, and is still in leadership, it couldn't be so bad for me to do it. I am only a sheep!"

Recently a number of prominent leaders have fallen into the sin of adultery. Some have left wives and married their secretaries without having any biblical grounds for divorce and remarriage. Sadly, I have heard unbiblical statements of repentance. "Well, yes, it was wrong, but God knows our weaknesses, and that I could not help it. I have asked His forgiveness and believe it is under the blood. We must be merciful if we are to have mercy." Yes, we are to be merciful and not exact revenge; but for mercy's sake we need to uphold biblical standards because we reproduce what we are. Leaders who are immoral and indulge sin will produce a church full of sin; a church without the fear of God and the power of God.

The truly repentant leader would say, "My God, what have I done? I left my wife and married another. I had no excuse to do so, for I had the power of the Word and Spirit to overcome my test. If only I had it to do over. I am stepping down from leadership. I do not know if I can ever be in leadership again. I must now make my new marriage work. For the sake of the glory of God, however, I must step down. I submit myself to my colleagues and to God that I might be of some use to Him in the future." That is repentance. It will surely meet with forgiveness, but not necessarily with restoration to leadership. *Forgiveness and restoration to leadership are two different things. One is the restoration of fellowship with God. The other still requires fulfilling the standards in First Timothy 3 all over again!*

American moral standards are at an all-time low. The church is the salt and light that should influence society to righteousness. We surely cannot do that as long as we understand mercy and love as indulgence and the abandonment of biblical standards. The standards of the

American Church regarding slander, gossip, lack of due process, adultery, greed and weird doctrines is astonishing. The world is in the church and the church has become "of the world."

Have we not learned that allowing sin in our midst can bring a judgment on the corporate Body? Israel was defeated at Ai because of the sin of one man. To be forgiven does not mean that we continue in leadership. It means that we can experience the love and presence of God again. It means that we will not be condemned to hell. It does not mean that God's standards for leaders in First Timothy are to be compromised. It is dangerous to violate the standards of God; it is more so in the New Covenant because we have more power to do His will. If we do not abide by God's standards and enforce church discipline, God will see that justice is done eventually. By then it will be much more severe and terrifying. Is that merciful on our part?

Our Young Need Moral Examples

We also ask for mercy and love for all of the young people and new believers who need to be discipled. The example of leaders is a primary discipling force. The purpose of God's Law is to direct us into the paths where real fulfillment is found. The ways which seem right to man often lead to destruction, as the writer of Proverbs noted. If we are truly merciful, we will seek to enforce standards. Then the sheep being tested will have the strongest possible example to motivate them to take the right path and find the fulfillment of God. To do otherwise is to be like the indulgent parent who will not discipline a child. True love overcomes the pain we feel in enforcing discipline for the good of the child. It is no different in the church.

The motive for seeking justice must be love and compassion, never revenge. Justice must be sought as a high, biblical priority. We must check our hearts to be sure of our motives. Then we must seek to follow the injunctions of the Word of God.

Hindrances to Love and Justice

Many people have a basic desire and an intuitive sense that there should be justice in the Body of the Messiah. However, the fulfillment of this desire is thwarted by false teaching and is discouraged by sin patterns among believers. That is in direct opposition to the meaning of biblical justice. We now look to expose these issues.

The Ends Justify the Means

It is generally accepted among believers that we believe in moral absolutes and not in situation ethics. Situation ethics is an historical position in ethical philosophy. This position was popularized by Joseph Fletcher in his book *Situation Ethics*. Many believers have not been trained in biblical ethics, an essential part of character development. They do not realize to what extent they act in harmony with an "ends justify the means" philosophy. For example, if they support ministers and organizations that have no solid accountability, arguing that they cannot pass up the good opportunities that follow from such an involvement (fellowship, sales of books and tapes, good preachers), then they are situationists. If they compromise with unethical leaders and groups for the sake of a false unity or of furthering some vision dear to them, they follow an "ends justify the means" philosophy.

In the classic Frank Capra movie, *Mr. Smith Goes to Washington*, the leading character battles against corruption in government. His former mentor, a leading senator, argues that his compromise with corruption was necessary to do many good things. So it is with many believers; the opportunity to extend their ministries causes them to compromise with those who slander, who are doctrinally off base, who lie, who have no real accountability and who are morally unqualified for leadership according to Scripture. Perhaps the event looks too important to pass up. Many important Christian leaders will be there! Perhaps it is an opportunity for television. So the unsuspecting person increases the influence of unethical people.

"Ends justify the means" thinking is really a denial of God. Only believers in God can hold to ethical absolutism; that ethical principles, understood rightly, are not to be violated and that cooperation with people who claim to be believers and yet grossly break ethical principles is wrong. God is the One who gives real, lasting fruit. We are never to calculate ends in such a way that illegitimate means become a possibility. There are innumerable factors we cannot see. We do not know what God will do in bringing opportunities to those who are true and loyal. What looks like a reasonable compromise for good ends might be just what cuts us off from greater blessing.

"There is a God in Israel." What does that mean? It means the believer can follow the principles of the Word even when it seems in the natural that the ends to be achieved will not be as beneficial. We do not have to lie, steal or compromise with evil for a good purpose. God will see to it that in the long run, real fruitfulness will be greater. We cannot always "see it in the natural," but we live in a supernatural world where God is ultimately in control.

Suppose "Rev. Smith" goes on TV with a shady television evangelist to publicize his book. He sees the importance of getting his word out. However, he has thereby given the impression of endorsing the shady televangelist. Others will conclude, "So-and-so televangelist could not be really doing so much wrong if Rev. Smith is on the show." Perhaps if Rev. Smith had stayed true to Scripture and departed from unethical people, God would have given him his own program.

It is always dangerous to calculate the beneficial ends that can result from compromise. Such compromise is, in part, a denial of the existence of God, or at least His control of the affairs of men. This problem is rampant in the church in America. The standards of Madison Avenue and its methods have permeated the church.

It is crucial that believers depart from situation ethics. *The ends never justify immoral means.* Justification in such cases is usually unbiblical rationalization.

Slander

Slander may be the most insidious sin that thwarts justice in the church today. In its worst form, gross slander spreads untrue, evil accusations against other believers. Marxists trained in disinformation learned that the truth of a matter was not important in discrediting an opponent. Instead, they found that if an accusation is repeated frequently and widely, it will eventually be believed by many. Slander and gossip is so pervasive among leaders and the average sheep that it is beyond belief. It may be one of the greatest hindrances to revival.

Slander destroys trust and tears apart the community of faith. Jesus prayed that we might be one (John 17:21).

He died to create a people of love and unity. In ancient Israel, the slanderer was required to receive the penalty for that of which he had accused another. Slander could lead to death. Slander is one of the seven things hated by God in Proverbs 6:19. It sows discord, according to that writer. It is a gross sin.

Slander has its origin in pride, competitiveness, power-seeking and insecurity. Strangely, these are all related traits. Discipline for gross slander should be severe, but we are indulgent. However, God included the bearing of false witness as one of the major "Thou shalt nots" of the Ten Commandments. Sadly, the person who engages in disinformation in order to discredit another (a greatly prevalent practice among leaders) often comes into deception and believes the lies in spite of the evidence. He may claim to discern it in the Spirit! It should be clearly noted *that the person who hears slander and gossip without strongly rebuking the slanderer and without initiating a process of correction is an accomplice to the crime and is thus guilty!*

What if the bad report is true, or partially true? Should we be silent when there is sin? Some would teach that we should look the other way and be silent. That too is wrong. Great sin and error among believers should be corrected. Yet that can be done only if there is due process. True accusations must be handled according to biblical standards of due process, not by private but accurate gossip! Gossip includes both false and accurate information shared outside the biblical order of due process.

Lack of Due Process

Without due process, the principles of justice are essentially compromised. The Bible provides the standards of due process for dealing with gross sin and error. Matthew 18:15 shows how it is done. It has been fully explained. When sin disqualifies a leader, the situation must be brought to the attention of those who can remove the person. In some cases, even when there is repentance, the matter will need to be made public.

Due process always requires that the accused have a fair day in court before the elders. There must be two or three credible witnesses. There must be a fair judiciary that believes in the principles of repentance and restitution. Furthermore, it is crucial that the accused have an opportunity to answer his accusers before the court and to bring witnesses for his defense. To deny the accused a fair defense before impartial judges is a travesty. Many congregations who seek to discipline try to avoid the painful process of allowing the accused his defense. The witnesses for the defense must be witnesses to the issues at hand; their testimony must be germane to the case. Judges must fairly decide their relevence. It is not a time to make irrelevant non-germane and non-substantiated charges against the accusers. Some who do not understand these judicial standards fear a fair defense and protect their leadership by not allowing one. That is wrong.

If the accuser refuses to deal with his accusations in a due process manner, the accuser should be disciplined for serious sin. If the accused refuses to deal with the accusations in a fair court, but responds by making counter-accusations and slandering to discredit his accusers, he must be disciplined.

The purpose of discipline is the healing and reconciliation of all concerned and for the glory of God. When the accused refuses to be accountable before a fair court of the Body of believers, it becomes right to make that known. The ultimate penalty is disfellowshipping.

It is important to emphasize that it is not wrong to share the information and conclusions of a fair court. If the brother or sister does not repent, it is biblically required that the sin and discipline be made known. Incredible as it might seem, some are so confused about these issues that they would consider the sharing of the decision of the court to be slander! Once due process has been followed, it is not slander. Instead it is a true but sad report that sometimes must be given to restore the Body to health and to cut off the unrepentant. At times even the repentant must support the sharing of the report of the court, that all might fear. That is the meaning of Paul's injunction to rebuke a leader publicly—that all might fear. Paul said some very negative things about some who were false and betrayed the gospel. We need only mention Alexander the coppersmith in this regard.

Condemning or Narrow Attitudes

Wrong attitudes are another hindrance to justice. Most matters of sanctification are ultimately between the individual and God. Yes, counsel and discipline are important, but only the work of the Spirit transforms. When we speak of justice and discipline, we are speaking of enforcing standards of doctrine and behavior that are the historic and unifying positions of the Church. These standards are clearly outlined in the Bible. Some would initiate the process of Matthew 18 and bring a case for every little thing. Some are so under the spirit of legalism that they enjoin harsh discipline for minor doctrinal and behavioral matters. These legalistic groups give discipline a bad name. They cause reactions and further anarchy.

A Wrong Concept of Forgiveness

A wrong understanding of forgiveness has been a major cause of the destruction of justice in the Body of

the Messiah. Forgiveness basically means to release
another from further indebtedness. When a person says,
"I was wrong, will you forgive me?" the example of Jesus
requires us to forgive. This forgiveness may require that
restitution be made by the offending party to prove real
repentance (the fruits of repentance). To say "I'm sorry"
can be a cheap way for a person to continue in sin and
be indulged by others. The manipulator will take full ad-
vantage of that. On the other hand, if the person is truly
repentant and the issue is not one of a sin pattern, the
offended party may release him from restitution. In
either case, the motive of the offended party should be
love.

The court of elders, however, should decide what is
just and declare it. Then the offended party may make a
choice. "Yes, I forgive you, but I do expect that, if you
are sincere, you will replace the car you took without
permission and totaled in an accident because you were
drinking." Or, "Yes, I forgive you, and because I know
you are sincere and this is not a pattern, I want to release
you from any responsibility to make restitution." The
court should advise when release from restitution is
detrimental to the person who sinned and to the honor
of the Name of God. Releasing a person, who unbiblical-
ly divorced and remarried, from child support is not
right for either the children, the spouse or the one who
divorced.

The biblical principle of forgiveness requires us to
give up personal hurt and the desire for revenge. We
must be free from desiring the other person to be hurt
because we were hurt. The motive of personal revenge
knows no limits. The offended party often is hurt
beyond the the normal reaction to the offense. That
proves the offense tapped into the stored-up bitterness
of a life of real or imagined offenses. No repentance or

restitution can ever be adequate for such a one. In the Middle East, a single killing means that the offended one will take revenge and wipe out a whole clan. Hatred can be a way of life.

The principle of forgiveness requires us to seek to receive the ability that comes from God so we can fully restore our fellowship with the one who did wrong to us. Our identification with the cross is a key to receiving the power to forgive. Forgiveness does not require that we trust; trust is something to be given to the trustworthy. Trustworthiness is proven over time. Forgiveness does require that we love and fellowship again, and that we take *small steps* of trust to allow trust to be built.

How often must we give such forgiveness? Jesus says seventy times seven (Matt. 18:22). In other words, the truly repentant brother or sister is to be received back again and again without limit. As a counselor who has worked with severely troubled people, psychotics, schizophrenics, etc., I have seen that being received is often necessary as part of their healing. They will sin again and again until the love and grace of God finally breaks through and delivers them. All of that has to do with what I call *forgiveness as a transaction.*

However, what if the person does not repent and has no desire to make restitution? Must we forgive anyway and act like nothing happened? I have three answers to this question. No! No! No! If the person has sinned greatly, a loving brother must hold him accountable. To let one "off the hook" is to encourage him in further sin. We are responsible for correcting a brother or sister in sin (Gal. 6:1ff) and to follow the due process of Matthew 18 if the sin is serious enough to require discipline. Truly, love does cover a multitude of sins in the ordinary course of life where we say the inappropriate thing or do something short of perfect love, etc. However, in matters of gross sin, for love's sake we must not let the brother "off the hook." The principle of forgiveness does not mean "business as usual." It may require that believers, who know of a due process decision of disfellowshipping, separate from the disciplined person. Forgiveness, as a transaction between the sinner and the one grossly sinned against, cannot take place unless there is repentance. Acting in love does not mean we are called to act friendly (in a "business as usual" way), as if there is nothing wrong.

Some will be shocked to read this. It goes against what has recently become popular Christian teaching. The old humanistic indulgence returns under the guise of "You must forgive me." Some unbelievers, like con artists, have claimed to be believers in order to literally "rip off" the saints, secure in the fact that the saints must forgive and take no action. Is that really so? The saints can disfellowship the rogue and take him to court so that society is protected.

Don't we have to forgive? I believe there is another meaning to forgiveness which is different from the transactional meaning. This forgiveness does not restore our fellowship with the sinning brother. However, it puts our hearts right. When we say "I forgive" in this sense, we mean the following:

1. I free myself by the power of God from all bitterness, hate and vengeful motives toward the brother. I receive this ability through the meaning of the cross of Jesus.

2. I release the offender to God so that it is no longer a matter of my mental preoccupation and a hindrance to my joy in God. If the person will not be accountable to due process in the church, or due process is impossible because of the substandard situation of the church, I need not have my life ruined by another's sin.

3. I receive love and compassion for the offender. My heart and prayer for the offender is for him to be fully redeemed or restored. Therefore, in compassion, I desire that the person come to true repentance.

4. Because my heart is loving, if the person repents, I will fully receive him back in the transaction of forgiveness.

This definition is a different but related meaning of forgiveness. It is *forgiveness as an attitude of love and compassion toward the offender.*

However, we must not be accomplices by encouraging persons to sin. Some teach a forgiveness that would do just that and allow the one in sin to minimize the seriousness of sin. Casting out the unrepentant sinner in First Corinthians 5 had the effect of awakening him to the seriousness of his condition. It brought real repentance. Indulgence through the wrong concept of forgiveness can be a factor in the destruction of another.

Forgiveness in either sense is not easy. A wife whose husband had fallen into adultery must overcome great personal hurt to receive compassion. Even when he repents, the transaction of forgiveness is not easy. This forgiveness means that the past offense would no longer be brought up in times of conflict.

Forgiveness does not mean that we give up our quest for a justice motivated by love and for the good of all.

The Assumption of Moral Equivalency

Assuming moral equivalence seems to be another major problem of modern people. In foreign affairs, the government that commits the worst atrocities is made equivalent to the one with imperfections. The Gulag of the Soviet Union (a huge evil) was equated with the jailing of Puerto Rican terrorists in the United States. These terrorists set off bombs that killed the innocent to achieve a national independence which the majority of Puerto Ricans did not want! Yet leftists spoke of both prison systems which held political prisoners as equal evils.

In situations of discipline, the argument of moral equivalence is often heard as a reason not to seek justice through due process or not to follow the concluding judgment of a fair process. For example, suppose a leader grossly slanders another leader. The innocent leader suffers years of discrediting in a concerted disinformation campaign. He has not been able to get the offenders to adhere to any fair process for resolution. In frustration, he lets the cat out of the bag that he believes the others are in sin. He calls for due process, but few will stand with him on this principle. Someone is always nearby to say something like, "Well, how can we claim they are in such sin? I have heard you speak negative things about them." Every person must fully repent of their sin. If one is only 5 percent guily in a conflict, he must still repent 100 percent of his 5 percent. Yet that does not mean both sides are equal in the dispute, or morally equivalent. The other might have to repent 100 percent of his 95 percent responsibility in a situation!

Often people assume that if there is a conflict, both parties must be equally to blame. Israel must be equally to blame for the lack of peace in the Middle East despite the wars started by the Arab nations. In my experience, it is very unusual to find moral equivalency in disputes. Usually one party is far more to blame than the other. However, there are some situations that are exceptions to this rule.

Another will say, "We are all sinners. You need to let God judge. We must just love, speak well of and cooperate with our brothers." Even if they are in gross sin?

Scriptural injunctions are quite different. They enjoin us to submit major disputes to fair judgment. All must have a fair day in court in order that testimony and investigation might disclose the truth. Perhaps one or both parties will have to repent of various sins and make restitution (to the church at large if not to each other). However, the assumption of moral equivalency destroys the possibility of justice. Until there is due process in a fair court, we don't know that there is moral equivalency at all. The one who refuses to submit to due process is guilty of sin; there is no moral equivalency in this case. *Almost invariably, the one who is willing to submit to a fair process of evidence and judgment is the one in the right.* Again, there are exceptions.

The one who refuses to pursue justice through due process and who is accused of gross sin against another or against Jesus the Messiah and His Body, should find that the rest of the church stands with the offended party. We should separate from those who will not resolve issues through due process. Otherwise they are encouraged in sin and empowered to continue doing evil. On the other hand, a party who claims to be offended but who will not submit his claim to fair judgment should not be believed, nor should his report be received if the other party is willing to submit to biblical norms. He should be confronted to handle his accusations biblically, according to Matthew 18.

Let us repent of the desire to be liked by all. Let us repent of all false teaching that leads us to *assume* moral equivalence between parties to a dispute. Yes, we are all imperfect. However, our imperfect actions are not the same as gross sin; our imperfections do not mean we are on the same plane as one who is in gross sin; nor does imperfection disqualify us from pursuing the injunctions in Matthew 18:15ff. All sins are not the same in weight. Scripture makes that perfectly clear. The penalty for refusing to repent of gross sin against God is hell, but even hell has different levels of punishment. Some sins are part of the multitude that love can cover. Other actions, which are not followed by repentance, require disfellowshipping.

The Wrong Definition of Taking Up an Offense

In Psalm 15:3 we read that one of the characteristics of a righteous man is that he is one who does not "take up a reproach [offense] against his friend." The teaching derived from this verse goes something like the following: "If someone does something wrong to someone else, it is between them. It should in no way affect my relationships. Therefore, I must continue to relate in the same way, despite the dispute the other may have." This interpretation of "not taking up an offense" counsels neutrality in every controversy. Yet this interpretation is not the meaning of the prohibition and is contrary to other, clear biblical texts.

First of all, taking up an offense means being bitter in spirit for another person because it is perceived that that person was wronged. This bitterness and offense is manifested, in a milder form, in distancing oneself from the one who committed the wrong. In a more severe form, it shows in speaking against the other who supposedly did the wrong. Sometimes that happens when the person himself who was supposedly wronged does not feel wronged or offended! The person who takes up the offense usually does so because of unhealed hurt and bitterness from the past. This past hurt is tapped into by more recent events and by their interpretations of those events. Wrongly taking up an offense should be defined as *becoming angry and bitter at one who supposedly did wrong without a righteous attempt to handle the problem according to biblical due process*. The heart is wrong whenever it is given to hurt and bitterness. The correction of a person in the wrong should always be motivated by compassion.

In the biblical order, sins committed publicly can be corrected by any mature brother or sister. If the sins are serious, it is judicious for elders to bring correction. Private wrongs should be handled by the offended party. Unless that person first sought to correct the one in sin, no one else should know about it. If such an attempt fails, then, according to Matthew 18, two or three others can be made a part of the process. Therefore, the one who takes up an offense in an unbiblical manner either shouldn't even know about it and has been part of a gossip transaction, or is not willing to be part of a redemptive solution to a public wrong. It is certainly wrong to take up an offense for one who will not deal directly with the one who did the wrong. Much gossip and sin in the Body is a result of gutlessness! In no case should there be gossiping or dealing with matters non-covenantly, outside of due process.

However, when one was sinned against seriously, when one who sinned refuses to repent or when someone refuses to be part of God's order for resolving disputes (such as being unwilling to submit to fair judgment in disputes) *believers are duty bound to stand with the one who is willing to do right*. Doing so may require separating from the one unwilling to seek reconciliation in a biblical way. That is the clear teaching of Matthew 18:15ff, of Isaiah 59 on the role of the intercessor standing with the grossly mistreated and crying out for justice, and of First Corinthians 5:11ff.

Believers sometimes get away with spiritual murder (gross slander)! Many of the sins in the Body could be prosecuted in secular courts, but are not because of biblical injunctions to not take a fellow believer to the pagan courts. It is good that we do not go to the secular courts. However, it is not good that there is little in the way of believing courts to see that spiritual murder is not allowed. There must be sanctions for serious sin.

Contrary to popular opinion, Scripture requires us to stand with the one grossly violated, with the one denied justice, and to separate from the one who refuses to act according to biblical norms of justice and due process. Doing so is not taking up an offense in the way precluded by the Bible. This separation is to occur only when attempts at due process fail. It is to be done for love's sake, not for bitterness, revenge or other such base motives. If we would understand that and so act, we would see much of the gross sin in the Body of believers addressed and handled. We could take a giant step toward cleaning up our act. To not stand against evil in this way is to empower people in their evil. It is to allow Satan to maintain his hold on the life of the one sinning.

Fear of Authority and Courts of the Church

Sometimes the lack of justice in the church is due to fear of accountability. A church court is a human, though divinely mandated, institution. It can err; it can be only as good as the humility, wisdom and spiritual maturity of the elders of the court. Therefore some have concluded it is better to leave all judgment to God. He will directly judge. Of course, such a thought is directly contrary to the biblical statements already presented in this book.

It is also true that a judiciary is limited by theological and experiential perspectives. It is therefore not helpful, for example, for non-charismatics, who do not believe in and practice the gift of prophecy today, to be judging error in the exercise of prophetic gifts. That can lead to gross miscarriages of justice. Prophetic practice needs to be judged by people of similar theological persuasion. Theological discussion among different communities is the prescription for differences of doctrine not defined in classical orthodoxy. Differences between Evangelicals, Charismatics, Pentecostals, Word of Faith people, etc., should not be decided by disciplinary courts!

On the other hand, it is better to have courts that make errors than to have no courts at all. God will raise up the truly humble and righteous if there is misjudgment. Indeed, the same argument could be used against courts in our society at large. That would be disastrous in society and is disastrous in the Church as well. It is a prescription for anarchy. There are safeguards that can mitigate unfair judgments and invalid disfellowshippings. (I have had direct experience with such errors.) In anticipation of the next chapter, it should be noted that only serious sin and doctrinal error should come to such court situations.

Secondly, although we are duty bound to take church discipline from other groups seriously, we are not bound to simply accept every decision of discipline at face value. For example, a charismatic would have a difficult time accepting the judgment of doctrinal error and disfellowshipping from a fundamentalist church where the decision was based on the view that exercising the gift of prophecy is wrong in principle and compromises the authority of Scripture. On the other hand, we should honor the disfellowshipping for unrepentant adultery where the evidence given under due process is clear. The fact that the adulterer might profess to be charismatic should not carry weight.

Differing theologies among those who profess biblical orthodoxy presently make it impossible that all decisions of discipline be received by all. Yet much can be done to support proper discipline from other groups. We at least should respectfully seek the facts and documentation for all discipline situations that involve us. God, with other ministerial flows in the Body, can vindicate one falsely judged. That is better than having no judiciary and waiting for God's supernatural judgment!

The fact that there is a plurality of denominations, independent churches and apostolic flows is a safeguard against the abuse of the principles of church discipline. Yet all should seek to deeply honor the principles of discipline and to support legitimate discipline wherever possible.

One of the hindrances to justice and discipline is the fear of shepherding, which I prefer to call "overlordship." I refuse to have biblical words stolen because some misused the words and gave them unbiblical meanings. Anarchy is not the answer to overlordship. We live in a lawless age that does not respect authority. It is not overlordship to have structures for church discipline, to enforce biblical standards for members and leaders, to seek counsel and confirmation from mature believers before making significant decisions before God and to disciple new believers. That is simply historic, biblical teaching. Theology formed in overreaction to error is bad theology.

What is overlordship? It consists in setting up an order of government in which the leader comes between a person and his God, so that the right of personal decision before God is precluded. That can be done overtly by the leader's asking to be followed as *the* voice of God to the follower. It also can be done by making social ostracism the price of going in directions contrary to leadership advice. An individual ultimately must be free to find the will of God for himself within the boundaries of the Bible's teaching on right and wrong. As important as counsel, confirmation and moving together as a congregation are, as part of God's order and wisdom, every person must ultimately weigh all counsel in his own closet of communion with God. People will stand before God for their decisions, in regard to what the Spirit says. It is our duty to see that structures of council, leadership and community do not compromise the principle of the individual's decision, in conscience, before God. We can require of another only what Scripture commands.

The issue of "overlordship" is sometimes raised as a smoke screen by those who do not want to be accountable in a biblical way. They resist the biblical injunctions of accountability, enforcement of standards, discipleship training and discipline. Such a smoke screen must not be allowed to obscure the fact that biblical justice is commanded for the church, and that the issue of overlordship is really a very different issue. Of course, extreme overlordship is a serious error that should be disciplined! On the other hand, there can be strong authority structures that do not violate the Scriptures. There is room for different structures of government within the biblical framework of due process and justice.

Narrowness in Moral and Doctrinal Standards

Some have a distaste for all teaching on due process, discipline and justice because the history of the Church sometimes reveals a lack of wisdom in their application. That is due to legalistic and doctrinal narrowness. Pre-tribulationists disfellowshipped the post-tribulationists. Today, without due process, pre-millennialists separate from amillennialists. In the nineteenth century, the closed brethren disfellowshipped the open brethren because they allowed non-brethren believers to share in the

Lord's Supper. Indeed, the Nazarenes in the early twentieth century disfellowshipped the early Pentecostals.
Speaking in tongues was considered to be of the devil
and thus a level of offense that called for disfellowshipping. All this discipline has caused a reaction and moved
many toward total non-discipline in the church today!

The solution for severe doctrinal disagreements
among those who profess the confession of classical
biblical orthodoxy is not to disfellowship. It is to pray
and seek the Lord to see if we first can be given the heart
to see in the same way. If we cannot, and the disagreement is severe, we should separate in an amicable way. It
is helpful to disclose the reasons. God is not pleased with
our need to separate like Paul and Barnabas, but He is
less pleased with our disfellowshipping one another over
offenses that are not biblically defined as major ones.
We can cooperate in significant ways and distance ourselves without slandering and disfellowshipping. Birds of
a feather, after all, will flock together. However, within
the bounds of biblical orthodoxy, God calls for greater
love and mutual acceptance.

The reformed dictum was, "In essentials, unity; in
nonessentials, liberty; and in all things, love." Severe discipline should be applied only in cases of gross doctrinal
or moral error, as clearly defined by the Word. I do
believe that the Word is clear in its standards. In addition, the history of the Church reveals a consensus for
understanding the standards of the Word.

There will be narrow groups. Human pride will always tend to legalism, to adding to God's standards and
to man-made laws. Human pride also will tend to anarchy. But that is no reason for us not to enjoin what Scripture requires. The historic and broadly understood
biblical standards for membership and leadership
should be established in our midst. A true manifestation

of God's order is the best safeguard against the extremes of both legalistic narrowness and anarchy. In the last days, the groups that disfellowship others who do not endorse the King James Version as inerrant will be a side eddy, apart from the broad flow of the river of God's moving.

John 17:21 Wrongly Applied

In a most glorious passage, Jesus prayed for His followers to be one as He and the Father are one. An incredible amount of "sloppy agape" (false love which is not love at all) has come from wrong interpretations of this verse, especially in the liberal, ecumenical churches and in the charismatic movement. There is a sense that, if we are to be one, all who profess to love Jesus (and among charismatics, those who claim to speak in tongues) are to be accepted. We are to overlook all doctrinal issues and indulgently forgive moral wrong (even if not repented of). Out of this broad-hearted unity, it is thought, revival will come. What incredible rubbish!

Will the Holy Spirit really come in revival for that which is full of sin and unholiness? Jesus did not pray that we would be one in an ecumenical salad, seasoned with gross sin and doctrinal error. Of course, we must overcome the barriers of narrowness and legalism to be one. However, Jesus prayed that we would be one as He and the Father are one. That is the oneness of a holy people who clearly affirm the great doctrinal truths that were once and for all delivered to the saints. That the verse of John 17:21 is used to thwart biblical justice, standards and discipline in the Body of believers is almost incredible and certainly tragic.

May this discussion of hindrances move today's church toward greater standards of love and justice.

CHAPTER V

ACCOUNTABILITY AND LIBERTY

We live in a day when, in the American Church, there is a wholesale departure from historic standards that once prevailed in evangelical Protestantism, including early Pentecostalism. This fact prompts us to ask the question of whether or not today's believers have discovered something that was not known in the historic church. Have they discovered a new meaning to liberty and forgiveness in the Messiah whereby the minister, having committed adultery, can continue in leadership? Have they really discovered a more wonderful meaning for grace? I do not believe so. Rather, I believe this departure reflects the general lawlessness in our society and the lowering of standards everywhere. The Church now reflects the world system and, like Hollywood, has its own version of "beautiful people" who are exempt from normal morality. There always have been lawless men and women claiming special revelation by which they could lead the people of God astray. One needs only to mention Thomas Muntzer of Luther's day. However, just as media experts dress up political candidates to deceive the public, so too they make Christian celebrities of renegades.

That the believing community does not rise up and demand biblical standards shows how far we are from the knowledge of God's ways. The words of the Psalmist in Psalm 119:136 are appropriate for our day: "Rivers of water run down from my eyes, because men do not keep Your law." Earlier, the same writer noted with great pathos, "For they have regarded Your law as void" (119:126b).

To establish God's Law on a basic level among His people requires that we adopt explicit and implicit biblical norms in several areas. To enforce these norms, we must establish courts in the church, understand and adopt biblical standards for leaders and members and remove members and leaders who no longer fulfill these standards. There must be clear processes for this enforcement. That clearly implies that we need to establish the meaning of jurisdiction. Jurisdiction defines where a person or leader is accountable. Jurisdiction defines the realm of the authority of a judiciary or a group of ruling elders. The discipling process should educate all believers in these principles.

Defining Jurisdiction

No one ever outgrows accountability to human representatives of God's Law. The teaching that a man in a head leadership position is accountable only to God is an evil teaching and a deception from the enemy. This false teaching has produced great destruction and division. A leader may have a headship role, but accountability to mature peers is necessary if standards of due process and standards of evidence from Matthew 18 are to be carried out. Failure to fulfill standards in First Timothy 3 requires removal. One who falls into a deception of gross sin or doctrinal error is likely in pride and unlikely to remove himself. Therefore, to protect the sheep, no one may ever set up structures that prevent their own removal, were they to become disqualified.

The principle of jurisdiction does not require a particular form of church government. Many types of government allow jurisdiction and accountability to be established. The primary judiciary in the New Testament is the eldership of the local church. Its jurisdiction extends to those who are part of the local flock and to those who are, or might be, affecting this local flock. This extension of jurisdiction is clear from the commandments to the elders of the local flock to guard the sheep from wolves and to exhort, teach and rebuke the sheep.

The principle of jurisdiction does not require a centralized denomination. It can be carried out from a structure as centralized as an episcopal system (governance by overseeing bishops who are mutually accountable in a college of bishops), to one as decentralized as an independent congregation.

This naturally raises the question of those who are in a parachurch ministry. It also raises questions concerning matters that are of an inter-congregational nature. At this point, let us consider the latter issue first.

Accountability in Inter-congregational Matters

My call for due process and accountability is relevant for those who believe in *completely* independent, local congregations. Under an eldership I do not believe that this type of church is the biblical ideal. Indeed, the biblical ideal is probably where congregations have such unity that they would be tied together in "a church of the city" eldership. This eldership then could handle inter-congregational (and inter-denominational) disputes. Cities could be linked to *ad hoc* groups; these groups could form to resolve disputes among congregations in various cities or regions. Leading fathers could serve in this way. However, the church today is too diverse in doctrine and practice to make such ties totally practical at the present time. There are several other ways to link judicial concerns beyond a local congregation.

First, congregations may be linked officially in an association or denomination. Their by-laws can include a process for appeal and for handling disputes that are either too difficult for the local congregation or that have implications beyond the local congregation (such as removing a leader who has regional, national or international influence). Congregations may be linked by apostolic connections to a pastor of pastors, who can bring elders together for such inter-congregational concerns. Lastly, *ad hoc* councils may be formed that can judge issues beyond the ability of the local congregation. Such a council of leaders beyond the local congregation can be called together because relationships among leaders are healthy. By-laws of the local congregation could specify the circumstances for and the means by which such a council would be called. My own preference is for an official linkage of autonomous, but not fully independent, congregations. However, because disciplinary matters sometimes affect other congregations in the same city, it is good to include representatives of other local congregations in those matters.

When there is an inter-congregational matter, because of the fragmentation in the Body of the Messiah, we need to recognize differences of approach and theology and set up structures whereby judgment will be given by others of like mind to the congregation involved. For example, it is not judicious for non-charismatics to judge an issue where someone is accused as a false prophet. The charismatic world has differences of theology concerning what would constitute a false prophet. In addition, there are different theologies on what the Bible teaches on marriage and divorce and on other issues. It is helpful if the theology behind the judgment is made clear. Then a person who was disciplined may freely join a group that would not have judged them on the basis of their standards. For example, in the Assemblies of God churches, a divorced person who remarries may never be restored to leadership. Another group, however, will believe in a process of repentance, counseling, restitution and restoration that could restore that person to leadership. However, that situation should not cause division between the Assemblies group and the group of the other persuasion as long as both are clear on their differences and both seek to uphold other basic, biblical standards.

Parachurch Organizations

Some parachurch organizations enforce clear standards and others, by their structure, allow for great abuse by the ministers who either lead them or are within them. Some such organizations believe they should have judicial jurisdiction over their workers and others do not. The church debates whether or not parachurch organizations are biblical. In the New Testament, it appears that members of apostolic traveling teams were accountable primarily to the leadership of the team. However, that does not fit the structure of many of today's parachurch organizations. I certainly do not wish to add fuel to the fire of this debate in this book. However, I do have some guidelines to suggest.

If the parachurch organization is to be a source of jurisdiction in church discipline, it must have an eldership structure. This structure would be a board of real elders who can discipline and who have sufficient involvement in order to have real authority. If the organization decides not to enforce such discipline over its leaders and workers, then those who work in it must clearly be under the jurisdiction of local congregations. The jurisdiction should be made plain to every member of the organization as well as to the congregations connected to the workers. It then will be the responsibility of the parachurch to uphold the discipline of the local congregations for its workers. On the other hand, if the parachurch claims such jurisdiction, it should make that clear to all its workers when they join. Its elders should know their responsibility and fully embrace it. Local congregations should respect the discipline of the organization if standards of due process are followed. In this latter case, the parachurch is really a kind of church with a specific mission. Local churches should be informed of the nature of this jurisdiction.

Every believer is called to be under clear jurisdiction. That includes all leaders. Woe to those who call others to be accountable to them, but who are not accountable themselves. No one should connect to any organization that is so ordered. In the New Testament, jurisdiction under eldership is established by baptism. In today's society, such jurisdiction needs to be made clear before baptism; a type of formal membership needs to be established. Without it, the civil government will not uphold the right of congregations to discipline. Losing huge lawsuits could result from not establishing standards and then trying to enforce discipline. This situation has already been tested in court. There needs to be a clear joining, and the one joining needs to be informed of his or her rights and of the processes of discipline and authority to which they are submitting.

What Is Mature Accountability?

The purpose of authority is not to exercise overlordship in the lives of the sheep. In its normal functioning, leadership is to equip the saints for the work of ministry. Everyone is called to some form of service. However, it is up to the sheep to submit for training and to respond to the Spirit concerning their calling. Beyond minimal standards of membership, it is up to the sheep to decide the level of involvement. Of course, leadership has the right to refuse a person who desires to undertake an area of ministry in the Body of believers, if the leaders believe that the person is unprepared for it. It is not wrong to remove someone from full "membership in good standing" for failing to fulfill basic membership standards of attendance, tithing, etc. However, when such is done, it is cause for exhortation, not for disfellowshipping. Transfers to other groups should make clear that the person's not being in good standing dealt with membership standards and not gross sin or error on other levels. Perhaps the new group will offer membership because it has different standards or will exhort the person to fulfill standards there.

Overlordship seeks to determine personal directions for the sheep's life rather than provide oversight and encouragement. Overlordship penalizes the member for not following advice which, although it may be good, is not a biblical command. It violates the principle of the person's responsibility to hear God's direction by the counsel of the Spirit given in the inner man. Although leaders have the right to order the life of the corporate congregation, and the sheep do not have the right to minister contrary to this ordering, the undershepherds of the flock have no right to dictate the personal life direction of the members. Shepherds are only to counsel and confirm in personal, directional areas. They should affirm people in their consciences when they disagree. One can affirm conscience without confirming a decision.

Our concern for discipline is not a call for overlordship. It is merely to enforce discipline in areas of sin that biblical teaching designates as gross sin or doctrinal error. Mature leadership is strong where gross sin and error are concerned, but always with the goal of restoration. Mature leadership is motivated by redeeming love. Mature leadership offers leeway to the members in regard to other issues. Mature leaders hold other leaders accountable to basic standards, but release them to creatively pursue the voice of God in their areas of ministry.

What Are Basic, Minimal Standards?

The question, "What are basic, minimal standards?" concerns what we affirm to be biblical standards. What are minimal standards for membership and for leadership? A group may have higher standards than these minimal ones and might discipline on that basis. Those who "buy in" make a covenant on the basis of those standards. Every group should make its standards clearly known. A group whose standards are less strict will not uphold another group's discipline on standards that are not shared. However, in shared areas, they should uphold one another. I am proposing here that the church agree on historic, minimal standards without which they cannot claim to be biblical.

Minimal Standards for Members

I believe that baptism usually should constitute provisional membership. That is not impractical in congregational settings. A minimal amount of instruction beforehand is adequate for ascertaining whether or not people are genuinely committing their lives to the Lord. If they are, it is not difficult to explain that a new believer is, in baptism, joining the company of believers under its eldership. The believer can transfer later to any legitimate congregation, if he or she so desires. It should be understood that when one commits to Jesus, he commits to the Body of Messiah and to the spiritual oversight of elders. That was understood in New Testament days. Baptism was joining the believing community of the city under its elders; it was an initiation rite of entrance into the community before community witnesses. Because our concepts of spirituality are so individualistic, the truth of this process has been lost to many. I believe we would see more solid conversions and much quicker discipleship if this pattern was followed. We would see baptism as a real key to testing the prayer of receiving Jesus. In baptism, we commit to Jesus as Lord and to *the pattern of life taught in the Scriptures.*

A true conversion is life-changing. If there is no change, the conversion is questionable at best. Historic denominations always asked the person to give testimony of how his or her life had changed as evidence of true conversion.

A true member is one who meets minimal standards of membership: not engaging in a pattern of gross sin, confessing true biblical orthodox doctrine in its classical sense and commiting to congregational life. Different communities may have additional, specific standards. The latter could include tithing, agreeing with the basic ministry thrusts of the community, being a regular attender of essential gatherings and serving in some area of Kingdom service.

A believer may fall from membership standards (even backslide) without being in gross sin or doctrinal error. That would cause him or her to become a suspended member or a "member not in good standing." In this case, pastoral involvement is expressed in encouragement toward a more serious biblical lifestyle or in encouragement to transfer to another congregation where the person could be more committed. Perhaps the present congregation just does not fit that person. Counselling should encourage the person to being committed somewhere. Perhaps temporary circumstances are keeping the believer back. Such situations demand our prayers, love and support. Our resources and time should be committed toward restoring.

Slipping from membership standards does not necessarily require disfellowshipping. Disfellowshipping is justified only when gross doctrinal error or sin requires it. To accept one as a believer in such a case discredits the gospel. If the person does not profess to be a believer, we are on different grounds and can relate to that person so as to win him or her to the Lord. The church is a place for struggling saints, not just perfected saints. Therefore, we need to bear with those who fall from membership standards (short of gross sin) and pray, counsel and exhort them toward full commitment.

The discipline of repentance and restoration, repeated over and over in the context of forgiveness, usually produces motivation to not go through it again. The repentant thief becomes tired of restoring what was stolen as well as a fifth! The slanderer will desire to stop gossiping, for his repentance and restitution greatly humbles him; all those he spoke to are contacted concerning his sin of gossip and slander and asked for forgiveness! The one who falls into serious fornication may show restitution by his willingness to embrace a discipline that shuns situations hard for him to deal with until after deliverance and the cross fully take effect.

Leadership Standards

The standards for elders and deacons in First Timothy 3 and Titus 1 are essential. Failure to meet these standards should preclude one from ordained leadership and governing roles. A continuous inability to live up to these standards should cause a person of integrity to voluntarily step down. If his peer leaders become aware of his failure to meet these standards, he should be asked to step down and if he is unwilling, be required to do so. We note that the standards of First Timothy 3 are based on relational success, which is based on character. No perceived measure of anointing should supersede these standards. Anointing can be used in witnessing and in non-leadership ministry contexts. God is serious about these standards because we reproduce what we are. Healthy leadership families reproduce in the community. (Leaders who are single should meet every other relevant criteria in these New Testament chapters.)

The nature of gross sin shows why fallen leaders need to be removed from leadership. Gross sin is not just a chance happening. There are almost always roots that can be as serious as the sins; roots such as loneliness, discouragement, an unhappy family life, unbelief, lack of intimacy with God and others, financial pressures and more. Unless these roots are dealt with, the sin is likely to repeat itself. A group of capable leaders should oversee a process of counsel and restoration. When they are confident of the person's healing and character stability, restoration to leadership is possible. *It is not loving to allow the fallen leader to continue in leadership after a profession of repentance.* Any sin which would, when there is no repentance, require disfellowshipping should also require a significant period of restoration for the repentant leader. It is an obvious implication of the character standards for leadership in the Bible.

Scripture requires that such sin be dealt with publicly. Doing so protects the flock and enables them to fear God. They know that leaders are required to live up to biblical standards. It engenders confidence. Furthermore, it protects the person from future discrediting if, after restoration, he resumes leadership. It can hurt the ministry when past skeletons, which once were hidden, are later revealed. I know of instances where leaders stepped down and were restored, but later on someone discovered the sin and publicized it. What is publicly known does not discredit a person with most people of good will, when proper repentance and restoration took place. However, when a person's resumé does not tell of the matter, some feel betrayed that they were not told; others lose trust. Gordon McDonald, the former head of Inter Varsity Christian Fellowship, followed this right pattern. He ministers today with great credibility and is a credit to biblical principles of forgiveness and restoration. I firmly believe that any significant public ministry in the five-fold ministries is subject to the principles of the requirements in First Timothy 3.

Financial Support

One reason ministers who fall refuse to leave the ministry is the lack of loving financial support. Many ministers have a support base in congregations; other ministers have built up a support base constituency through years of service. They do not see any way they can adequately support their families were they to step down. They are not trained for other professions. Some would say that such ministers lack faith. That is callous; at such a time faith often is at a low ebb. That is where the love of the Body of the Messiah is so important. There needs to be a financial support base to make up the difference during the time of restoration or to enable a transition to another profession if the leaving of full-time ministry is to be permanent or long term. I believe a local congregation can, at the least, continue a part-time salary for a year. Congregations should cooperate to establish funds for this purpose. Otherwise many will choose to continue in ministry out of a sense of necessity to support their families. That is wrong. It is also wrong if the church does not lovingly support its fallen but repentant ministers. If the church is serious about enforcing standards, the church also needs to be serious about the compassion that is part of restoration.

Divorce and Remarriage

Standards required for members and leaders that concern divorce and remarriage are a source of great controversy today. First of all, churches, associations and denominations are not united on what constitutes biblical standards for divorce and remarriage. Secondly, churches are not united on whether or not a restoration to leadership is right for one who has either a legitimate or an illegitimate divorce and remarriage. Indeed, many congregations do not recognize their responsibility to issue a letter or certificate of divorce with the right to remarry if they do believe there are legitimate grounds for such.

Denominations that believe there are never grounds for divorce and remarriage do not allow for any divorced and remarried leaders (even if the people were divorced and remarried before they became believers). When someone who has been divorced and is remarried comes to another group from such a denomination, the new group needs to find out the circumstances of the divorce and remarriage.

Those groups that believe there are legitimate, biblical grounds for divorce and remarriage need to issue a clear policy statement to define these grounds. Then, when a case of legitimate divorce with the right to remarry according to their standards does arise, they need to issue a certificate of divorce detailing the grounds for their decision. If they do not issue such a certificate, and there is a divorce and remarriage which leads to discipline, they need to issue a statement of the grounds of their discipline and document that due process was followed. That will enable various groups to be aware of the standards involved and the reasons for the elders' decision. It can enable others to make an informed decision as to what level, if any, they can be involved with the divorced and remarried leader or member according to their own standards.

All groups that seek to uphold biblical standards should be able to agree upon the need for any divorced person to step down from leadership (for whatever reason a separation or a divorce is effected). Even if one spouse initiated and received a secular divorce against the will of the other partner and against the standards of the congregation, the relatively innocent party still should not be in leadership. Why? Divorce is a traumatic experience. A person who has been divorced is in no condition to continue in leadership and certainly does not fulfill the family requirement standards of First Timothy 3. Such a person, in my view, may requalify by these standards, either in single life or in a new marriage. However, even if the divorced person is not in sin, he or she needs to requalify. That will take a significant period of time. Health reproduces health; the newly divorced cannot be in a good position for biblical leadership. It is amazing to me that such an obvious implication of biblical teaching is missed by so many in today's church.

In rabbinic Judaism, binding and loosing is understood to include the responsibility of issuing a certificate of divorce when legitimate. That certainly is the implication of Matthew 18, with regard to the responsibility of eldership.

One of the greatest sources of division in the church today is the receiving of disciplined leaders by a new group, thus thwarting the process of restoration. If a group's standards are less strict than the disciplining group (but still reasonably defensible in the light of Scripture) that can be made clear. A person under discipline who repented in word and deed may, after a period of time, desire to transfer to this other group. He should then be free to do so. However, a period of restoration should still be enjoined by the new group. Communication between the two groups is important. Standards of First Timothy 3 should be met in the context of the new group if the person is to return to leadership. If the standards of the two groups vary greatly, the group with stricter standards must decide, in conscience, what level of involvement they may have with the other group and the former leader. Two cannot walk together unless they are agreed. However, if there is no continuation in gross sin, the two groups can at least live amicably in the same area.

In regard to divorce and remarriage, the following standards are held variously in the church today.

1. There are no grounds for divorce with a right to remarry, ever. Therefore, to divorce and remarry in some groups leads to disfellowshipping or, at the least, a permanent preclusion from leadership.

2. Divorce with the right to remarry is legitimate if a spouse is in unrepentant adultery, repeated adultery, homosexual sins or other gross sexual sins.

3. Divorce with the right to remarry is legitimate according to the previous statement (# 2) and for the grounds of desertion by a spouse, according to

First Corinthians 7. In such a case, the deserting spouse should be disfellowshipped.

4. Those in this category agree with the grounds enumerated in the second and third statements and add the following proviso: A divorce may be granted in exceptional cases where a spouse has abandoned the marriage in covenantal responsibilities, even though he or she continues to live in the same house. This type of divorce is very exceptional and should be handled with great care before the elders grant it. The partner who abandoned the covenant should be disfellowshipped (sometimes wife-beating, drunkenness and other types of severe sin like rebellion, abuse and psychological abandonment, are included).

5. Some accept the grounds enumerated previously (#2—#4), but add the following ground: Though both marriage partners are believers and try as best they can, if they simply cannot get along, it is better to divorce than to build up bitterness. God's forgiveness is such that these persons should be allowed to remarry.

I do not see how any Bible believer could come to the conclusion of the last point (# 5) while taking Scripture seriously. However, those who grant divorce for this reason (and there are some evangelicals who do), should make the grounds clear so that others can know where to stand. Scripture makes it plain that two truly born again believers always have the resources in God to make their marriage work, if they are willing.

Standards for divorce and remarriage should be part of the written policy of every congregation. By issuing their standards and the grounds for specific decisions in divorces, with the documentation of due process, the air can be cleared. Then each group can decide how it will relate to the divorced person by its own standards, even if those standards differ from the group that originally issued the decision. In addition, a person can transfer later to a group with more lenient standards, if he so desires. Other groups can choose by their standards whether or not to receive such a person as a leader. At the least, knowing the truth of the matter helps us decide with clarity according to conscience. But today, great confusion reigns in this area.

Our community does not allow those who are, according to our standards, illegitimately divorced and remarried to be members or to minister among us unless there is full repentance and restoration according to our understanding of the Scriptures.

Restoration

Can one who has grossly sinned be restored not only to membership but even to leadership? Can one who has illegitimately divorced and remarried be restored to membership and to leadership? If restoration is possible in such cases, what would constitute adequate repentance, restitution and restoration? This question is a cause for great controversy between congregations. May God restore our unity.

Among Bible believers who believe in discipline and restoration, there is no real consensus concerning the issue of restoration. Almost all believe that a person can be restored to full membership. God's unconditional love and forgiveness restores any truly repentant person. *However, this love must not be construed as indulgence. It is not an "anything goes" philosophy.* Generally, truly repentant people desire to do all they can to right the wrongs they committed. They work to restore the reputation of the one slandered; they seek counselling to restore a broken marriage; they repay stolen money, plus additional compensation.

Because most believers do not understand that the biblical concept of repentance includes restitution, many have been hoodwinked by Satan's emissaries. People are received back into fellowship because they say "I'm sorry." One professional con artist, who professes to be a believer but is not, travels throughout the country to believing communities and fraudulently "rips off" the saints. When caught, he says "I'm sorry." He has no intention of paying back his victims. He believes he has the saints over a barrel because, by his profession of being a believer, they cannot take him to secular court. We are to be wiser than that. A court of the church needs to disfellowship him so that believers may take him to the civil courts. Only if he proves his repentance by working on restitution can the Body accept him as a believer. When Zacchaeus repented, he restored all that was stolen. Then Jesus announced that the Kingdom of God had come to his house!

A person who has grossly sinned needs to prove his repentance with fruit before being fully received back into fellowship. There can be a probationary acceptance until that repentance is shown to be real. The number of times a person may sin and repent in word and deed and be received back is not limited. Love may cover a multitude of lesser sins, but gross sins or capital offenses require a demonstration that the repentance is real. A loving community will do all it can to aid the individual in showing the reality of repentance, including prayer, hugs, encouragement and even helpful direction in making the steps of restitution. However, significant steps of restitution must be made.

Concerning membership, we affirm that restoration to the Body of believers and to full fellowship is open to all, no matter what the sin.

What of the person who divorced and remarried without biblical grounds? This area is one of the more difficult issues. Can the person be restored to membership? I believe it is possible, but only if repentance is real. Many statements show no repentance at all and negatively influence the quality of marriage commitment among the saints if allowed. Compare the following two statements of repentance:

1. "I know that what I did was wrong. However, God knows our weaknesses. I simply came to the end of my rope and temptation overcame me. However, God is forgiving and knows I couldn't handle remaining with my former wife, and that my new wife was one I truly needed."

2. "Yes, I divorced and remarried contrary to Scripture. I had no excuse to do so, for Scripture promises the power to do the will of God. I brought disrepute upon the gospel. Would that I had it to do again, I would not so sin. However, the teaching of Scripture now requires me to make the second marriage work."

The first statement is not biblical repentance at all. We even have heard some say that Scripture must not be used legalistically, but that the Spirit led them to divorce and remarry because God knew their call to be exceptional.

What would restitution be in such a case? The proof would be repentance before the spouse and the children, responsible child support if children are involved and a lifetime profession of the truth. This profession requires that the person never justify the action, but consistently profess to have missed God's will in the act of divorce and remarriage. Testimony to the grace of forgiveness is not wrong if it is in the context of such clear restitution. The profession of the truth is part of this restitution. By this truth, other couples will be motivated to work on their marriages when conflicts arise and to not easily bail out.

Can a person in such a situation ever lead again? Some communities believe that such a person can never fulfill the standards of First Timothy 3 because there are two living spouses and there were no biblical grounds for divorce and remarriage to the second spouse. Others believe that a person may show fruit of repentance, and that over time he can be restored to leadership. I won't try to settle this issue. However, a truly repentant person in such a case will not continue in ministry or even return to ministry in the near future. At the least there must be a stepping down from leadership, a significant period of restoration, a proof of real restitution and a clear re-fulfillment of standards in First Timothy 3 (recognizing that restoration in this case, if a group allowed it, would imply an interpretation of First Timothy 3 whereby a person can be qualified by his present marriage even if there is a living, former spouse).

Many use the "call of God" idea as grounds for not enforcing discipline. The call may well be there, but so are the character qualifications. That call must wait for the more important issues of character and for relational accountability to be established before entering back into the call.

Other than in the difficult area of interpreting passages on marriage and divorce, most would agree that God can restore anyone to membership and leadership, no matter what the past sin. However, trustworthiness needs to be re-established. That often takes a number of years. If restoration takes place, the past cannot be covered up. Whether or not restoration to leadership is expedient for the sake of God's Kingdom is important as well. What is legally acceptable may not be expedient for God's Kingdom.

The Principle of Transfer

Every citizen of our nation is under the jurisdiction of the courts established in the land. No citizen is ever beyond the jurisdiction of the courts in his local area and the special courts that handle special issues (e.g. tax courts). In the same way, every believer comes under the jurisdiction of the courts of the Church. Eldership is responsible for lovingly encouraging, teaching, counseling and correcting. This same eldership is responsible for enforcing discipline in cases of severe covenant violation. This concept is no new thought; it was the historic position of the Church.

Many parachurches do not establish the nature of their jurisdictions. Many people find ways to fall between the cracks of jurisdictions. The American Church in not understanding the principle of jurisdiction, has contributed to an "anything goes" mentality among American believers.

Most believers are plainly to be under the jurisdiction of a local congregation's elders. It is crucial that these elders be trained in their judicial responsibilities in addition to their other functions.

Jurisdiction is maintained over the life of a believer by the eldership of a congregation where he or she is a member until he or she is *transferred and received* in another Bible-believing congregation. I do not believe that it is correct for an individual to simply resign membership. The exception to this rule is when the local congregation becomes cultic and will not transfer to a Bible-believing variety of congregations (Charismatic, non-Charismatic, Independent, Presbyterian, Methodist, Messianic Jewish, Free Church, Lutheran, etc.). If another group does not understand or practice the principle of transfer, the first congregation can maintain contact and some jurisdiction until the brother has joined the new group. The first can contact the second group and seek to communicate in such a way that a valid change of membership can be effected. Hopefully the new group will be just if a question of severe moral sin or error is at issue. Of course, no transfer to an unbelieving group can be effected. A congregation can then carry out their discipline, but also recognize their limits if the backslidden believer joins a church in heresy or anarchy. Hopefully, through discipling, believers from their midst will want to join only groups that practice the principles they share.

If jurisdiction and discipline are to have a more significant effect, it is crucial for congregations to respect the principle of transfer and to seek to uphold the discipline of the church wherever possible. Any member in good or not in good standing, as long as they are not under discipline for gross doctrinal sin or error, can and should be freely transferred. The witness of the Body of the Messiah is compromised, however, when for various reasons, other congregations receive those who are under discipline for gross sin or error.

When people come to a congregation from another connection, it is crucial for that congregation, through a leader who has authority, to initiate communication with the first congregation. "Is there any reason we cannot receive the brother or sister?" If the issue is gross sin or error, the new congregation should seek documentation to establish that the first congregation acted with due process and clearly established the case. On the other hand, the new congregation can provide a check on unreasonable discipline by the first congregation. For example, "overlordship groups" will disfellowship members for failing to obey the leaders in areas of personal life direction, for failing to adequately tithe or for other errors which are less than extreme. A new congregation usually should seek to uphold the discipline of the first, but is not bound to do so if the discipline is found to be unfair by biblical norms. The discipline of local congregations is to be respected, but is not absolute in a way that would establish tyranny.

It is important to destroy the competitive spirit between congregations. This spirit causes us to be too ready to believe the worst about another congregation and to believe a negative report from a new member who transfers. We should always seek the facts, even if the congregation is one which we do not trust. If to our knowledge a congregation is in decent order, and is a Bible-believing group, it may be wise to see if the reason for transfer is that significant. Perhaps a leader can restore the person to his or her former congregation and help clear up problems. Imagine the trust and unity that would grow! Francis Frangipane, an Iowa pastor and leader in fostering church unity, requires in most cases that a potential transferee return to his former congregation for at least one month. During this month, that person is to offer intensive, daily prayer for the pastor, leaders and the congregation. Afterwards, if the potential transferee still desires to change congregations, Pastor Frangipane will work with the other congregation to effect a godly transfer.

It is obvious that the establishment of good relations among congregations of various denominations and apostolic flows is important and needs to be pursued. Good relations among congregations who care about integrity fosters love and justice and hastens the day of the Lord's return. It can lead to joint efforts among congregations for more effective evangelism and even change our communities, cities, counties and states!

Establishing Courts of the Church

As I have stated, the elders of a local congregation are the first and primary court for most people. If a parachurch has a genuine board of elders to which it is truly accountable, I do not object to its having jurisdiction. However, that jurisdiction needs to be made clear. If leaders in both groups are trained in their judicial functions, these courts will be adequate for most issues (I believe 95 percent of the issues that arise).

Some issues can arise that require inter-congregational courts. Disputes between congregations in the same denomination or apostolic flow can be handled by an inter-congregational eldership in the association. Sometimes the disciplining of leaders is too hard for the local eldership and also can be handled in this way. I believe, too, that it is very important for denominations and apostolic flows to provide at least one level of a court of appeal. The appeal court can decide whether or not there is sufficient evidence for an appeal to be heard. Cases that have significant translocal implications can be heard here as well. This can provide stability and greater confidence in the decision of the lower court.

When issues arise between congregations or movements that are not in the same denomination, flow, etc., these issues can be handled in several ways.

1. Churches of a locality may subscribe to an inter-congregational court to hear such issues. This court is composed of leading elders of the city who can deal objectively with these issues. Following this process could begin to restore a perception among us of being part of one Body, that is, the church of the city.

2. An *ad hoc* court can be established to which both sides of the dispute submit. This court should be

comprised of men of experience and wisdom who are trained in judicial responsibility. Both sides would agree to its composition.

3. There may be need for specialized courts for issues too difficult for elders trained under normal circumstances. Issues that deal with complex financial and legal matters may require a group for mediation that understands these complex issues. The Christian Legal Society seeks to provide a court of arbitration for such issues. The elders responsible for the members involved should be fully aware of the proceedings and should be involved where they can in such cases.

Apostolic Teams and the Authority of the Church

For those who believe that there is a continuing function for persons who perform apostolic functions (overseeing multiple churches, pastoring pastors, directly planting new congregations or indirectly aiding in the planting of new congregations), I desire to share some insight into the relationship of these people to what is being taught here. We do believe in apostles, with a small "a," defined as performing the functions previously listed.

We believe that appeal courts under apostolic leaders can aid the cause of justice greatly when issues are between congregations. Furthermore, under joint apostolic leadership, appeal courts can be formed to handle disputes between flows of congregations. Actually, the reason a parachurch can have jurisdiction biblically, in my view, is the Scriptures showing members of apostolic teams as being accountable primarily to the team and not to a local congregation. In this case, however, the parachurch is well served when overseen by a true plurality of elders who understand their function as an apostolic team responsible for its members. Although local congregations can minister to the needs of apostolic team members, it greatly eliminates friction for such parachurches to define and clarify jurisdictional boundaries. It also will aid local congregations where such team members attend. Biblically, there is no parachurch without eldership jurisdiction (in the sense of non-church). There are, simply, two kinds of church expression: one is local congregations; the other is trans-local ministries whose members are under the authority of the leadership of these apostolic teams.

In the intensity of these last days' deceptions, persecutions, false prophets and wolves in sheep's clothing, can we afford not to establish justice in the church? Satan seeks to destroy congregations as a first order of business. He uses those who lie and say they are believers when they are not. If we do not establish justice in the church, we will be sitting ducks for Satan's attacks. He certainly seeks to divide and destroy through slander. Immoral leaders are another inroad. Leaders and believers with significant weaknesses can lend themselves to Satan's strategy.

Justice cannot be established without due process and the restoration of courts to the church today to handle such matters. That is one way wolves in sheep's clothing can be exposed and lose their influence. Unless the moral standards of the church of the last days are high, we will be unable to stand firmly in faith in the day of battle. The breastplate is the breastplate of righteousness! Righteousness and justice are related concepts, stemming from the same Hebrew root word! Justice is simply the order of God's righteousness described by Scripture. That we are entering an age of intense tribulation is no excuse for avoiding these principles. The early church established its courts in the midst of great persecution and turmoil.

I understand that God's restoration of the church in the last days will produce a situation where greater prophetic knowledge and greater direct interventions by God will establish fear and holiness (such as in the case of Ananias and Sapphira). Direct intervention in judgment is not God's only method. As Paul needed to call for the establishment of courts in First Corinthians 6, and as Acts 15 manifested the work of the court, and as we understand the meaning of eldership, we certainly will need to work to establish the courts of the Church as part of God's way for establishing justice. His severe interventions will also come, but the establishment of due process and justice can prevent a more severe judgment from falling on many when His last days' judgment begins with the household of God. To simply wait for God to judge directly is neither biblical counsel nor merciful.

CHAPTER VI

PRACTICAL DIRECTIONS FOR THE CHURCH

(A Summary to This Point)

Structure alone does not overcome problems. People of character in positions of leadership are necessary. On the other hand, leaders with great character can at times transcend inadequate structures of authority. This book makes it clear that biblical structure makes room for leadership to exercise gifting, but that leadership should never be without accountability. *Checks and balances* are part of the orientation of the Bible!

To fulfill the ideals of this book, several commitments are crucial for the entire Body of believers to adopt. It is time for the charismatic movement in many quarters to repent for rejecting classical, historic standards because of a reaction against denominations. Denominations sometimes did develop centralized and stifling structures. However, the denominations also had many positive benefits. Not everything in the denominational structures was wrong. It is time for us to re-evaluate historic church structures and to ask questions of what is worthy to be fostered today. The anti-denominational stance of many comes from pride and leads to structures that are without justice or biblical order. The following are the commitments that the church today needs to make to recover God's order of justice.

A. Commitment to Leadership Standards

It is time for today's church to commit to the leadership standards of First Timothy 3 and Titus 1. The only way discipline can be enforced is for each congregation and its leadership to commit to these standards and to set up structures of accountability whereby any leader who falls, and thus no longer fulfills these standards, can and will be removed.

Another part of establishing discipline requires those who are in traveling ministries and who are sent to establish new congregations or ministries to be truly accountable to an eldership of integrity. This group must be committed to the biblical standards for leadership and should vouch for the character and the adequate preparation of the minister covered. During the planting stage, these elders should hold the planter accountable to leadership standards and financial integrity. Until such time as a planter raises up elders in a new congregation, such channels of accountability should remain. In New Testament times, recognized leaders gave letters of recommendation which were carried by traveling ministers. Can we do less today? It is time for the people of God to know the biblical standards for leadership and to make sure they are submitted to leaders who fulfill these standards. Doing so will be one significant check against authoritarian abuse. All members should know the proper way to bring charges against leaders who are in serious sin or error.

B. Commitment to Membership Standards

The need for minimal membership standards is crucial. A true seeker might not be living up to the standards for believers. However, once he professes to be a truly born again believer, he needs to be challenged to come into full membership. That can be done as part of baptism or shortly thereafter, when membership instruction has been given. A potential member needs to know his responsibilities as part of the congregation and his relationship to the elder of the congregation.

A congregation cannot allow one to profess to be a true believer in Jesus and yet live in gross sin or foster serious, basic, doctrinal error. Secondly, to allow these professing believers to remain connected to the congregation in a limited way, without real commitment, is to discourage the commitment of the whole community. It is time to build communities of faith that seek to reflect the Kingdom ideals taught by Jesus and by the apostles. It is time to stop building a weekly rally as a substitute for true Body life. A "McDonald's drive-in" religion is not biblical. A radio or television "church" is not a church!

C. Commitment to Establish the Courts of the Church

The principle of the eldership in each local congregation having a judicial function needs to be firmly established. Congregations need to truly desire and pray that elders fulfill their full biblical function.

The principle of the courts of the Church needs to be taught to the members; they need to see what the eldership court is for and how it is to be used.

It is also important that courts be established to settle inter-congregational disputes where at all possible. At least local congregations can have provisions in their by-laws for *ad hoc* courts to be established for such disputes if they are not connected by either denomination, apostolic flow or congregational network to such a court of appeal. Courts of appeal are also a check against abusive structures of severe "overlordship," which can develop in local churches.

D. Commitment to Train Elders for Their Judicial Responsibilities

It is crucial for elders to be trained in their judicial responsibilities. Such training, first of all, would include understanding Matthew 18 and the biblical process of correction. It is also crucial for elders to be trained in clear knowledge of all the New Testament passages concerning their judicial function and of how to practically apply these passages.

It is important that elders be trained in biblical law and in how to apply it in the New Covenant order. All of the Bible's instructions for judges and for the establishment of justice need to be fixed in the hearts of the elders. Elders need to learn how to weigh evidence and testimony. They need to be given practical examples of restitution that would fit various offenses. This training needs to fully examine the difference between biblical love and justice and "sloppy agape." They need to know that rendering fair judgment, without favoritism, is a high biblical calling. Furthermore, they need to clearly understand that making a judgment on the basis of the evidence rather than simply calling for superficial reconciliation is very important.

Eldership requires the fruits of the Spirit. Patience and wisdom are part of that judicial temperament that is necessary to the functioning of the courts of the Church.

Elders also need to realize that they are responsible for issuing divorce certificates where justified and to refuse where not justified. The penalty of congregational discipline should be used when a divorce without biblical justification is pursued. Indeed, an unwillingness to be reconciled to a spouse or to another member in good standing in the Body of believers is grounds for discipline. The New Testament community is a community of forgiveness and reconciliation!

E. Commitment to Resolve Disputes

It is time for us in the Body of believers to grow up. That means we are to seek to resolve our disputes in a spirit of love. Unless there are overwhelming convictions of conscience for separating from a community (or communities), we should submit to the decisions of the judiciary under which we are committed. Perfect justice and love are not to be expected in this life. Fostering wounded pride is sin and one of the greatest sources of division in the Body of the Messiah. Therefore we need a deeper commitment to carry out the decisions of the elders, rendered as part of the process of arbitration, instead of requiring a decision that fully confirms one's own position. We need to foster such deep commitment as highly valuable and only disobey when biblical principles are clearly violated. Commitment to avoiding splits is biblically enjoined.

Unless there is gross moral sin or error in the leadership, the decisions of elders in resolving disputes should be accepted and submitted to for the sake of peace. Forgiveness, repentance and restitution should be offered according to the wisdom of the elders' decisions. Even society, in general, requires a certain level of resolution before the civil courts of our land. Can we require less in the society of Jesus?

Of course, the disunity of today's church concerning doctrinal matters means that disputes in many areas need to be judged by those who do not come from a vastly different doctrinal perspective. Although they come from vastly different perspectives, those who believe in the judicial function of elders would resolve some issues in the same way. These would be in areas of more universal doctrinal and moral agreement among believers who believe in congregational discipline. However, many issues are not of this nature. Sometimes disputes arise that seriously divide people, even though the issues are not capable of clear determination by universally held norms of doctrine and behavior. In these disputes, judges need to share the basic theological thrust of the participants. For example, how should disputes be judged which arise from mistakes in prophetic ministry?

It is important for judges to issue clear decisions that include their evaluation of the rights and wrongs in the situation. If they believe that minor issues are being given too much weight, they need to state the issues and the reasons that is so.

F. Commitment to the Principle of Disclosure

When leaders fall, there are feelings of hurt, confusion, disappointment, betrayed trust and crises of confidence. The greater the prominence of the minister, the more serious the fall. We might also note that, to the extent a ministry truly makes a godly impact, the more serious the attack of the devil to discredit the gospel. How is confidence and faith restored? It is by making public the basic facts of the sin (not the lurid details); the discipline that has been enjoined by those who hold the fallen leader accountable and the process for possible restoration. Possible, not certain, restoration to leadership is in view because those who hold the leader accountable must affirm that standards of First Timothy 3 have been reattained as a prerequisite to leadership.

We believe in restoration for wounded and fallen soldiers. However, we believe in a process of restoration that reflects Kingdom principles. Public disclosure clears the air and restores confidence! It is so simple; why do so many not know it? If sheep were wounded in the situation, pastoral counseling and inner healing need to be available to the sheep.

Disclosure also has a reference to an open structure of government. Congregants and constituents should know where funds are spent. They also should know the vision, direction and policies of the organization through congregational gatherings, available audited summaries, written statements and other means.

People who give should know that they are responsible before God to know for what they are giving. This knowledge must not be difficult for them to attain.

G. Commitment to the Principle of Transfer

The world is full of professing, "Lone Ranger" believers. They live contrary to scriptural norms. It is crucial for every believer to be established in the community of faith and to know where their accountability is. It is crucial for every leader to establish the same for his life. It is time for the Body of the Messiah to return to the historic standard of transfer as explained in the last chapter. These standards show the truth that all believers are to be accountable and under elder jurisdiction. That jurisdiction remains until a person joins another congregation, apostolic flow or team.

Summary

May God grant that these commitments become universal in the church in the days to come. I believe these commitments are necessary if the Body of believers is to mature and deal with the many wolves in sheep's clothing the enemy will send into our ranks in the last days. Fair processes of justice will protect the truly innocent and will ferret out the wolves.

CHAPTER VII

ILLUSTRATIONS REVISITED

We now return to the illustrations from the first chapter and apply the principles that were discussed. The reader may want to review the illustrations from that chapter.

Illustration # 1

The lack of shared, basic standards was a major weakness in the pastors' fellowships. For both this example and the next, I cannot too strongly emphasize that a pastors' fellowship should at least be based on minimum covenant standards. Such standards include: seeking to uphold the discipline of other congregations where such discipline adequately followed standards of due process; refusing to receive bad reports outside of a clear, Matthew 18 process and affirming a covenant of good report (which is crucial in such fellowships, otherwise they are easy prey for Satan).

Of course, hindsight is easier than foresight. Therefore these next comments must be taken as offered with great empathy for Pastor Nelms, the leader of the fellowship.

In no way should the new pastor, Pastor James, or his pastor guest, Pastor Jacobs, have been allowed to share gossip and mistrust concerning the association of congregations to which Pastor Nelms was relating. Pastor Jacobs should have been cut off in his accusations and asked some pointed questions. With regard to his accusation of a hidden agenda, he should have been asked for proof of such. If he did not have any, he should have been rebuked for bringing his mistrust into the group. Secondly, his accusation of "overlordship" should not have been allowed. Once that word had been mentioned, he should have been asked if he had sought to approach those leaders with evidence concerning overlordship. If he had done so, then had he sought to approach them with other leaders? What was the nature of the evidence? Was the leadership group involved given a chance to answer their accusers face to face, with Pastor Jacobs as a witness? Or did Pastor Jacobs simply receive evil accusations against these leaders?

Those who leave a congregation sometimes make many unfounded accusations. However, when checked, most accusations fall to the ground. Satan is the great accuser of the brethren. It later came out that one accusation of "overlordship" came from two men who were told they were to no longer share an apartment. They shared their anger at this intrusive shepherding. What they did not share was that they had a homosexual relationship which had come to light and was the cause for their discipline.

Illustration # 2

The issue of a pastors' fellowship needing standards applies to this situation also. Our introductory comments for the first illustration apply here as well. However, the fact that evidence was presented to seven national leaders should have been sufficient cause for the pastors' fellowship to stand behind the discipline.

The leader from New Hope Church who was under discipline had a national ministry. Therefore, it was not wrong to ask people with whom they were in relationship on a national level to confirm discipline.

On the other hand, the lack of local leaders in the discipline confirmation reflected local relational weaknesses, which undercut people's willingness to uphold the decision at the pastor's fellowship. Still, that should not have caused the members of the pastors' fellowship to have such a difficult time accepting the principle of upholding discipline. Indeed, discipline should be received as valid if it follows basic due process principles. It was wrong to make such a major issue of the lack of the involvement of other local leaders. If we can reasonably give credence to a court of the Church, in this case, an *ad hoc* court, we should!

Unfortunately, Assembly of God pastors accepted the principles as valid within their own denominations but could not see applying basic standards in a trans-denominational fellowship. That was a great lack. Should we eat with unrepentant adulterers or murderers at a pastors' fellowship? Shall we not ask those who judged the issue if repentance and restoration took place? The standards of discipline enjoin us to not eat with such a one. That is for all believers; it is not limited to being applied as, "Do not eat with such a one in your denominational context."

Pastor Jacobs led a large charismatic church and on that basis was given credibility. He was a part of recommissioning Pastor Wilkens. He and Pastor Wilkens claimed that due process was violated by the counsel of seven. Fellowship representatives could have at least investigated and questioned the counsel of seven to ascertain if due process was followed.

The size of Pastor Jacobs' church should not have influenced other pastors when he gave bad reports and did not follow due process himself. He needed to be corrected like anyone else. Searching questions on due process and real evidence should have been presented to expose his unbiblical action. Unfortunately, many believers are still overly enamored by large size and external success. Of course, all of this advice would have been difficult to follow; the pastors would have had to been taught the principles of Scripture at the same time they were being asked to take scriptural action.

Until pastors' fellowships accept the principles of discipline and covenant, they will continue to be either fellowships of unrighteousness or weak fellowships that are easy prey for the devil.

Illustration # 3

This illustration shows us the devastating results of a congregation being structured so that the head leader is not accountable. It is true that the other leaders were stymied by the legal structure they had allowed. On the other hand, it was their responsibility to follow Matthew 18 and to seek to remove Pastor Simms. They should have approached the head leader as a plurality of leaders and demanded that he step down. All of the congregants should have been informed of the situation and called upon to follow the other elders. The building still might have been lost, but the congregation could have been saved. Perhaps even the building could have been saved.

The biblical commandments concerning discipline supersede any constitution or by-laws which contradict them. The by-laws of this congregation voided the commandments of God. The national association should have publicly exposed the situation and called upon the leader to give the assets to the ongoing congregation. Doing so could have informed the former congregants while encouraging them to follow the other elder leaders. Following these steps might not have worked; but this kind of pressure might have moved Pastor Simms.

Illustration # 4

Because the Church today is so lacking in judicial process and righteous discipline, a case like this one is difficult to resolve. Yet it is important. It seems plain that the disfellowshipping congregations acted with due process and according to historic standards. The radio station and the host of the show that featured James Scott claimed that it was not their responsibility to deal with such issues; they were not a church. That is foolishness. As believers, they are responsible for biblical norms. Therefore, to give the name "Christian" to a station and to allow leaders under discipline to use it as a platform is to undercut that discipline. The directors of the station were responsible as believers to uphold the discipline of the church. It is that simple.

It is true that human charisma and continued ministry will enable one to eventually bypass discipline standards in today's American Church. This is because the church is so lax. If a leader believes he was falsely disciplined, he should seek a court of appeal to hear all the evidence. It might lead to his exoneration or to the confirmation of the disciplining group. Even if there is disagreement between the two courts, at least it becomes clear to the Body that there is another reasonable perspective. Furthermore, any trained leader should recognize the difference between real repentance and the false repentance which says, "We are all sinners and

God has forgiven me!" Yes, He has forgiven if you have *truly* repented. The idea of continuing in leadership under such circumstances is unbiblical, notwithstanding the example of David. Read the account of what happened to David's family and to Israel after his sin. Is that what we want to invite upon the Body of the Messiah? The New Covenant calls for higher standards because we have the power of the Spirit.

Due to the lack of a consensus on standards and solid court structures, some are restored by God and truly repentant for the past without any clear decision having been rendered. In these cases, we may, until God has restored His Church more fully, have to rely on the fact that the confession and profession of repentance is truly a biblical one. "I was wrong, I had no excuse." Then there should be other leaders who can vouch for the stable and holy life now being lived. Furthermore, we should look for the leader to relate to elders in such a way that there is real accountability. Until the church of today is restored to standards, some of the past may need to be overlooked to get on with the future. This future should find us maintaining biblical standards.

A leader disfellowshipped like the one in this case should at least make the grounds of his divorce clear (or his interpretation of the Bible's standards on divorce and remarriage). Doing so would dispel confusion and allow people to decide to support his ministry or not, according to their own biblical convictions.

Illustration # 5

How sad that men enter into covenants and yet so easily break them! A leader who is under discipline for serious sin and is given a just direction for restoration should not be trusted if he opts out of it. It is not only the sin of adultery or other gross sin. He is a covenant breaker. No one should receive the ministry of this person until he goes back and carries out the assigned discipline of restoration. If due process was followed, if a covenant bond of accountability was established and if the standards for restoration were basically reasonable for re-establishing standards of First Timothy 3, then all believers should stand together against the brother continuing in ministry. Neither the believing public nor other leaders should undercut discipline by supporting or endorsing such a leader.

If we would respond rightly, the person would be forced to take the right spiritual medicine. In the process of counseling and sharing, the root causes of sin could be dealt with. In the context of covenant restoration, loneliness would be avoided and *true restoration* could take place. The denomination could have called upon the believing world to support their discipline.

I realize there are cases where a man is in a denomination that does not believe in restoration. He may, in good conscience, be led to another credible group to provide this restoration. However, a quick re-entry into ministry destroys both his and the group's credibility. Gross sin is evidence of major weaknesses that take time to be addressed. Establishing that First Timothy 3 is fulfilled takes a significant period of time.

One of the most abused Scriptures is the statement in Acts 5, "We ought to obey God rather than men" (v. 29). The context surrounding this verse is the authorities forbidding the disciples to obey the explicit command of Jesus to preach the gospel. How sad that many use this quote as grounds for disobeying elder authority in a process of accountability, restitution and restoration! "The Spirit told me I am restored; I am accountable to God, not man; I must obey God rather than man." These

statements misuse Scripture and are nothing but rubbish. Yet how often we have heard such Bible-twisting in
the mouths of the rebellious!

Illustration # 6

In this case we have both a lack of biblical action by
those who should hold the fallen leader accountable and
a lack of right response by those who presumably know
the inside story.

That is a key point. We do not know that Rev.
Howard Johnson really fell as was reported. How do we
know there was no discipline? Indeed, ministers "in the
know" are responsible for bringing their evidence to the
leaders of the association and for holding the association
accountable in applying biblical discipline. This discipline should include a public disclosure of the facts
and the process of restoration that is to be followed.

If the association is in sin by failing to bring discipline, (as in the case of Eli the priest), then a group of
mature leaders who know the facts should, after having
approached all levels of confrontation, *officially* disclose
their evidence and the judgment they believe Scripture
requires.

I do not believe that Scripture always requires us to
cut ourselves off from the leaders who refuse to fully discipline, provided there is some discipline, however inadequate from our point of view. However, if there was
no biblical discipline, how can we avoid the principle
seen in the Hebrew Scriptures: a city that allows gross sin
is itself to be punished by the other cities? I believe that
allowing gross sin (for example, unrepented adultery or
theft) without any repentance or a restoration process
would require us to separate from the indulgent organization. For some, the fact that the sin is exposed and

counseling and restitution ensues, though the minister continues in ministry, will be seen as adequate for maintaining fellowship with the group. That would, at the least, require some assurance of real accountability and of the fact that the minister is not continuing in sin. For others that would be too tolerant; they would break fellowship. I would maintain fellowship with people in the association, but certainly would not join or participate in the functions of an association that is so lax. I would urge stronger biblical standards for the association. However, if they continued to support one who fell into repeated sin, I do not see how anyone could biblically do anything but separate in such circumstances.

If the rumor is true, that the association did not discipline the fallen leader, then the association is in a place of serious sin. The association certainly should deal with this sin up front by public disclosure and the announcement of discipline. The rumor may be false, and if it is false, then, sadly, mistrust of the association and its leaders was spread.

Illustration # 7

Two possibilities exist for this case. The leader who is being accused, Rev. David Spock, might or might not have fallen as the friend claimed. However, David Spock claims to have never fallen in this way. The denomination involved does not believe in restoration for fallen leaders. In addition, the denominational leaders profess to have made no decision concerning the leader that they will disclose. When asked if there was a past disfellowshipping, the leaders say only that there is no present decision against the leader. They will not disclose any past sin.

It is possible that the denomination involved is remiss in its responsibilities. We may never know. However, since there is no documented evidence as part of a due process conclusion to prove that Pastor Spock fell, and since he professes that he did not so fall, the bad report is a rumor. It is sin to spread this report. Since his ministry bears good fruit and shows a solid family life, it would be wrong to separate from him on this basis. The same is true in the case of the friend's report against Jack Bixler. Without due process, nothing was shown, especially by rumors of twenty-five years ago.

Because today's American Church does not discipline properly, we sometimes find ourselves in puzzling situations that are far below the ideal. Some ministers fell, truly repented and over the years showed a godly life. They did not have the benefit of biblical discipline and restoration. They were not connected to any structure of leaders that would properly restore. It is possible that they even stayed in ministry over this time. If their lives show years of stability, good fruit and a reflection of standards in First Timothy 3, I can accept that God did a work of restoration. God is the Restorer; human beings are the instruments. The fault belongs to the Church as a whole for the processes being such a mess. Some have been restored by God without due process because they genuinely sought God. Others who continue in ministry produce havoc because they opted out of biblical processes and standards.

Although we might accept ministers who truly repented without a more biblical process, that is no excuse for continuing to neglect biblical order in the church today. Every minister should be connected to others intimately acquainted with him and who can vouch that standards of First Timothy 3 are being fulfilled. "Truly, these times of ignorance God overlooked, but now commands all men everywhere to repent" (Acts 17:30). The reader is no longer in ignorance now. God commands us to seek to uphold biblical standards and to join with those who will.

Illustration # 8

Competition is a huge nemesis in the Body of believers. Ministries compete for people by seeking to offer the best product, not so much to win the lost, but to effect the lateral transfer of believers to them. That is serious sin before the Lord. Because of this spirit, we believe the worst of our brothers who are in leadership when disgruntled people whisper in our ears about them.

We seek to have the best show in town. It is amazing to note that, according to the advertising in a national Christian magazine, many large ministries each host the most important conference for everyone. Since many of them are scheduled for the same time, it is hard for the believing public to decide which of *the* most important conferences they need to attend. Conferences can be times of significant training and inspiration. However, conferences generally are not the most important events on the face of the earth today.

In the particular case here, the competing organization's leaders were only too glad to receive a bad report about the other organization and its leaders. They violated Scripture by receiving the brother without hearing the side of the slandered executives. This second group never checked out the divorce issues. The slandered executives might want to peruse the issue of the immorality of the other organization's receiving and spreading bad reports or slander. However, competition is so intense, it may not bring a cooperation that would effect reconciliation. At least the behavior of the sinning organization should be made known after due process.

Sadly, many believers choose their involvements by the goose bumps raised and not by the integrity and justice of the organization. Would to God that we would experience goose bumps when we see integrity, righteousness and justice! How can we bring justice to the nations when we are so full of injustice?

Illustration # 9

Competition is again the root of the problem in this situation. The competition and kingdom-building continues because others in leadership allow it to continue. First, the leaders of the organization that is sinning should be confronted according to Matthew 18. If they are not willing to repent, other leaders and believers should withdraw their support from the activities headed by the sinning leaders. Gross slander is serious.

In addition, many need to see that the biblical requirement is not to "refuse to take sides" or to "refuse to take up an offense." We have shown that attitude to be a false interpretation of Scripture. Rather, Scripture, for love's sake, requires us to stand for justice and due process and to withdraw from those who reject those biblical standards. By feeding the monster of pride through support and cooperation with those in this sin, one never sees the monster slain. Pride is slain when it does not gain its ends. The withdrawal of support would have a great effect, if not on the sinning leaders, at least for the Kingdom of God.

Scripture requires us to stand with those denied justice, with those who are abused and mistreated. It is especially applied to the poor who are so often exploited by the powerful. If we would so stand, the Body of the Messiah would see true love expressed in relationships and reflected in biblical norms of righteousness. The

Law of God is the expression of the love of God and of one's neighbor. Where His Law is violated, love is surely absent.

Illustration # 10

The error in this case is seeking to protect the fallen leader through privacy. As this case shows, covering up the sin of a fallen leader is contrary to Scripture and often backfires after the minister resumes ministry. The skeleton in the closet is somehow discovered and taken out for all to see. The right thing to do is to disclose the sin and the process of restoration undertaken, thereby clearing the air. Future unrighteous accusers are thwarted by the records and public knowledge of the truth, which is now part of the leader's resumé and testimony of God's grace to restore.

It is never too late to follow this process. As soon as this truth is understood, the leader should seek to document the facts and gain the signatures of those who were involved in the discipline. He can than make the truth clearly known.

Illustration # 11

The ability of leaders to believe the worst in this case was amazing to me. No one should have believed the evil reports being spread. Biblical norms would have required us to ignore the reports unless Matthew 18 was followed. Following biblical injunctions would have led to a believers' court case to hear all of the evidence. Those who sit as elder judges in such a court need to take the time to hear all of the evidence as well as the rebuttal. Then a judgment should be rendered.

Accusers who refuse a fair court for decisions usually know that their case will not hold up under a more objective examination.

In this case, the accuser confused the people and other leaders by claiming that he followed Matthew 18. It is true that there were meetings of the first step. However, he never made it clear that he was unsatisfied with those meetings, and that he was initiating the next steps in the process. At the third stage, a constituted and capable eldership needed to hear the whole case. Red flags should have flown in everyone's mind because there was no clear documentation or proof that those later steps outlined in Matthew 18 were accomplished or even properly attempted. The profession of following Matthew 18 by the accusing leader was a false profession.

I want to make it plain, however, that once Matthew 18 is violated, and a severe dispute arises, it is no longer right to go back to the first steps of Matthew 18. It has become publicly known and is affecting many people. When this circumstance occurs, the applicable Scripture is First Corinthians 6. According to that passage, we are to appoint judges to hear the issues, with full evidence and testimony, and to render a decision. Men influenced by the evil one will seek to prolong a dispute indefinitely so that, by delaying tactics, evil might prevail. By word of mouth, the slander continues to be spread. One of the key norms of justice is that it be rendered swiftly.

Many leaders do not understand the norms for evidence and judgment. Judgment must not be subjective or intuitive. Some leaders do not want to take enough time to hear all of the evidence and to properly deliberate. They believe they do not have the time; their ministry responsibilities press upon them. The process could take several days, but important inter-congregational cases are well worth the time. The lack of such structure and judgment has taken far more time and energy from key leaders than a few days in court. Judges need to understand their role according to the principles of the Bible as recounted in this book.

The situation we now speak of was investigated by Samuel Leslie. That was helpful, but inadequate. Those who made the accusations still needed to face the ones they accused before a fair court. Until then, the doubts concerning the accused and the accusing leader, Pastor Clements, will be widespread in the church. Some of the air was cleared by the investigation, but not all of it.

The Church has a responsibility in love and justice to confront the accusing leader as well, that he might avoid a more serious judgment from God; especially if he is making false accusations. It seems that we find every way we can to avoid objective courts under qualified elders! Only a fair and full court of the Church can clear the air.

Conclusions

In these last days, God *will* have a people that fulfill the prayer of Jesus in John 17:21, that we be one as He and the Father are one, so the world will believe the Father sent the Son.

This oneness will be achieved when we are filled with His Spirit, and from this filling we become intensely committed to His righteousness and His compassionate love. This oneness will be a product of God's full restoration of the equipping ministries in Ephesians 4:11ff, and as part of that, an eldership according to biblical standards. The equipping ministries will train the people toward maturity. The eldership members of the equipping ministries will give themselves to enforcing God's standards of righteousness and ensuring the standards of First Timothy 3 for leaders. The eldership will assume their proper judicial role when required. That includes judging fairly in disputes, receiving and granting of

transfers, issuing statements on divorce and remarriage
and disciplining (even to the point of disfellowshipping
where necessary). This eldership will be a band of
mutually accountable leaders who are motivated by the
Good Shepherd's heart of love for the sheep.

As of 1992, American society is in a crisis. Heinous
behavior is protected by law. Laws protecting the family
and fostering traditional values have been jettisoned.
Believers have failed to influence society toward
righteousness and justice. The Reagan years were not a
return to biblical norms. There were only a turn to traditional economic ideas, motivated by the financial set-
backs of the Carter years. It was not a moral revival. The
rate of teen promiscuity is at the highest level in our history, despite AIDS and a host of other venereal diseases.
The reason for this situation is not the evil of the secular
humanists and the New Agers. It is, rather, the power-
lessness of the American Church. Because the church
has been a society that allows serious sin in its midst, we
cannot turn our nation around. Only a just society, the
church as a righteous counterculture, can affect our
society in the right way. Only the concerted effort of
multiple congregations in a locality can turn the tide.

We are called to be the salt and light of our society.
Salt is a preservative and flavoring. What is the condition of the American Church? The classical denominations have largely apostasized. The major exceptions are
the Southern Baptists and Missouri Synod Lutherans.
The American charismatic world is without clear standards and is tainted with scandals and non-account-
ability; the evangelical world is affected as well by this
crisis of standards, but less than the charismatic world.
We have allowed the world system to influence us. Evangelicals lack the power of God. The fundamentalist
world is still largely isolated from engaging society and
embracing their brothers in the Messiah because of a

legalistic narrowness. A mighty revival is greatly needed to turn us to righteousness.

This revival has begun in movements of church planting in America and in the third world. Hundreds and even thousands of churches that are moving in power and holiness are not famous in the media. When the religious empire of greed, competition and injustice falls, we will see the church of the twenty-first century arise. It is a church of righteousness, justice, holiness and power in the Spirit, and is burning with compassionate, God-inspired love.

APPENDIX I

LETTER OF TRANSFER

Name of Congregation
Address of Congregation

The Board of Elders
Covenant Community Church
City, State, Zip

Dear Fellow Elders (or Pastor, or whoever is to be addressed),
Mr. and Mrs. (or Mr., Mrs., Miss) are (is) presently members in good standing of our congregation. We hereby transfer them to your oversight with our full recommendation.

Yours in His Service,
Name for the Board of Elders

_____

- - - - - - - - - - - - - - - - - - -

Please mail this form when you receive (name) into membership so that we may be released from our responsibility.

Name of Congregation _____
Address of Congregation _____
_____

We hereby do notify you that _____
has been received into the membership of our congregation.

Signature _____

Office/Position _____

APPENDIX II

TRANSFER WHEN
NOT IN GOOD STANDING

Name of Congregation
Address of Congregation

The Board of Elders
Covenant Community Church
City, State, Zip

Dear Fellow Elders (or Pastor, or whoever is to be addressed),

We hereby inform you that (Mr., Mrs., Miss,) _____ _____ is a member, but not in good standing in our congregation. The reason, according to our standards for membership, is _____ (e.g. lack of attendance, financial support or service, or whatever other reasons would be related to the situation). We do not have any official or pending discipline with regard to gross sin or doctrinal error toward (him, her, them). We will therefore transfer (him, her, them) to your oversight with the recommendation that you seek to exhort (him, her, them) in these areas of concern.

Yours in His Service,
Name for the Board of Elders

Please mail this from when you receive (name) into membership so that we may be released from our responsibility.

Name of Congregation _____
Address of Congregation _____
                         _____

We hereby do notify you that _____
has been received into the membership of our congregation.

                         Signature _____

                         Office/Position _____

APPENDIX III

REFUSAL OF TRANSFER

Name of Congregation
Address of Congregation

The Board of Elders
Covenant Community Church
City, State, Zip

Dear Fellow Elders (or Pastor, or whoever is to be addressed),

We hereby inform you that we are unable to issue a transfer for (name or names). Our refusal is due to (enumerate gross sin or doctrinal error involved) _____

_____ .

We have carefully followed the process of Matthew 18 for loving confrontation and hereby enclose the records of our confrontation, testimony, evidence and our decision of (pending or completed) disfellowshipping. Please cooperate with us and work with the involved person(s) that (he, she, they) may be either reinstated into our membership or transferred to your charge. Please contact us so that we may work together in a redemptive way toward (his, her, their) restoration.

Yours in His Service,
Name for the Board of Elders

_____

APPENDIX IV

LETTER OF DIVORCE

Name of Congregation
Address of Congregation

The Board of Elders
Covenant Community Church
City, State, Zip

To Whom It May Concern,

We, the Board of Elders, of (name of congregation) do hereby issue this letter of divorce to (full name of person). We believe they have the following biblical grounds for divorce with the right to remarry:

_____

_____.

We have examined the evidence of this situation according to biblical standards of evidence and testimony.

This letter grants the right to divorce and remarriage only upon obtaining the necessary right issued by the civil government for divorce and remarriage.

Sincerely,
Names _____

_____

_____

The Board of Elders

MEMBERSHIP CATEGORIES

The goal of recovering classical membership standards in a practical way has been fostered by our adopting the following categories in our membership rolls. We offer them to you for your consideration.

1. *Provisional Members*: those who are newly baptized or are newly transferred from another congregation. They have been given basic instruction before baptism concerning the fact that baptism is initiation into the community and a coming under eldership oversight. What this entails, with regard to discipline under the elders, if there is gross doctrinal sin or error, should be made clear. Such instruction can be done in a very brief time period (a half hour to an hour). Provisional members commit to seek full membership as part of their profession.

2. *Full Membership in Good Standing*: those who have completed the membership book either through the membership class or through homegroup leader oversight and self study. They are regularly attending, tithing and serving.

3. *Membership Not in Good Standing*: those provisional members who fail to fulfill full membership standards after a reasonable period of time or full members who fall from full membership standards for a period of time.

4. *Under Discipline*: those either disfellowshipped or presently in a process of discipline for gross doctrinal error or sin.

Those in categories one, two and three can be transferred and their status explained to the new pastor. Not all provisional members will remain where they were first received. Only those in category four should not be transferred.

APPENDIX VI

PROVISIONAL MEMBERSHIP

At Beth Messiah Congregation, we believe that a person who is immersed in the name of Yeshua under our auspices or who transfers to Beth Messiah should be immediately received into *provisional* membership. In New Testament times, immersion was understood as joining oneself to the corporate community of believers under the Lordship of the Messiah. This included coming under the authority or spiritual oversight of the elders of the community. Your acceptance of immersion or your transfer to Beth Messiah is a commitment of provisional membership which includes a commitment to seek *full membership* here or to transfer to another Bible-believing congregation, and a commitment to accept the spiritual oversight of the elders of this community. This is similar to joining a nation and receiving citizenship. In this, one comes under the governing authority and the laws of that nation.

Eldership oversight at Beth Messiah includes praying regularly for members, giving counsel, biblical teaching, training for spiritual service, correcting according to the written Word and disciplining for gross sin or doctrinal error if members fall away from the Lord. If one claims to be a follower of Yeshua while continuing in gross sin, one can be disfellowshipped. That means the members of Beth Messiah will be told that the person is to not be accepted *as a believer*. We want all who either are immersed in water by us or who transfer their membership here to understand that civil courts in the United States have especially noted that congregations must make their standards clear to potential members before they have any right to enjoin biblical discipline.

We believe that eldership authority *does not* include requiring a member to order their personal life directions in accord with eldership counsel. Elders can only require that which Scripture clearly requires. Beyond basic membership standards, all members must be free to follow their conscience and the leading of the Holy Spirit for their personal life directions. We are committed to the importance of counsel and confirmation as part of congregational life, but are also committed to safeguard our members against abuses of authority. One of these safeguards is our commitment to transfer any member, who is not under discipline for gross sin or error, to any Bible-believing congregation.

The step of immersion or transfer is a step of joining a special congregational family. What a privilege it is to serve one another together in the Kingdom of God!

APPENDIX VII

GROSS DOCTRINAL ERROR

One of the great problems of today's church is defining gross doctrinal error. This lack of definition has produced strife at levels beyond belief. Why? Leaders are willing to define gross doctrinal error as "whatever does not agree with my interpretations." Far too much is defined as essential and therefore becomes a basis for severe criticism of other ministers and groups. For example, we have seen extraordinary and slanderous criticism of other leaders and groups for the following reasons:

1. They believe in inner healing.
2. They believe in inner healing in the wrong way.
3. They do not believe in the *any moment pre-tribulational* return of the Lord.
4. They believe that the gospel we preach is the gospel of the Kingdom.
5. They believe that believers can have a demon or be demonized (not possessed).
6. They do not believe in a literal millennial age wherein people would still be living in earthly bodies, marrying and having children after Jesus returns (this view of no literal millenium is called amillennialism).
7. They believe in the integration of true insights in psychology with Christianity as helpful to counseling.
8. They believe the Holy Spirit teaches us, through life experience, things not *directly* in the Word.
9. They believe that the latter rain movement was of God.

10. They believe that there are saved Roman Catholics.
11. They do not believe that prophets or those who exercise prophetic gifts must be 100 percent accurate.
12. They believe in dreams and visions from the Spirit.
13. They believe in positive confession of the Word to build faith.
14. They believe in the restoration of the function of apostles and prophets in today's church (not in the sense of giving new doctrine).
15. They believe in a last days great harvest.
16. They believe in influencing society politically.

And so on, and so on.

In my view, none of these issues are reasons for lambasting and discrediting other ministers or ministries. Usually those who harshly denounce others over such issues do not represent the view of the other fairly. Indeed, it is a cardinal rule of fair criticism that we do not attack personally, and that *we represent the other's view to his satisfaction before criticizing*. If we cannot do that, we have no right to criticize. Dialogue in a good spirit through conversation and writing can aid in our finding truth; denunciations over these issues accomplish nothing. Furthermore, none of the listed issues involve gross doctrinal error sufficient for separating from other brothers and sisters.

Gross doctrinal error is defined by the classic creeds of the church which are summarized in such statements as the one put forth by the National Association of Evangelicals. A group can define their official association more narrowly, but should not be engaged in denunciation of those who do not share the more narrowly defined perspective.

We ourselves, at Beth Messiah and at Tikkun Ministries, define our association of congregations with explicit statements that describe what we believe about Israel, Jewish calling and the last days. Yet we fellowship with people who do not see all of our distinctive affirmations on these points.

Those who believe in the classic doctrines as: the full inspiration and authority of the Bible (as the final and full authority of doctrine), the deity of Jesus, the triunity of God, the substitutionary atonement, resurrection and ascension of Jesus, His second coming and final judgment, are our brothers in fellowship. If they seek to test doctrine by the Word, we can act as brothers even if we have differences on many issues.

Discipline for gross doctrinal error and public denunciation of wrong teaching should be limited to those areas considered classic doctrines. Other areas where we differ may be a reason for our going separate ways (different vision, approach and interpretation), but should not be grounds for public denunciations, disfellowshippings or other ungodly modes of response.

TIKKUN MINISTRIES

Tikkun is a Hebrew term that means "restoration." It reflects our burden and belief. We believe Scripture teaches that the Church will be restored to power, love, unity and righteousness. This renewal will be a key to the restoration of the Jewish people and their ingrafting into "her own olive tree" (Romans 11). We believe that the last days, according to Scripture, will see a progression of events leading toward the full restoration of Israel and the Church. As the Church is restored, we will see a significant number of Jews saved and a continued return of Jews to Israel. With those Jews who are the saved remnant of Israel, the Church will intercede and witness in love until Israel turns to Yeshua. Romans 11 is a key passage of last days teaching. Tikkun Ministries is committed to seeing these restorations come to pass in the last days.

As part of our vision we are engaged in the following ministries:

1. Training, sending out and supporting congregational planters in the United States, Israel and other countries.

2. Fostering Jewish ministry in local churches.

3. A full-time Bible and graduate school for training leaders for the Jewish vineyard and for work in the Church.

4. Sending out teachers and preachers for conferences, evangelistic campaigns, services in Messianic congregations and churches, etc.

5. Sponsoring music and dance ministries.

6. Helping to bring about a consistent pattern of unity with the Body as an expression of our deep conviction.

The leaders available for the above ministries include Daniel Juster, who is the Chairman of the Board of Tikkun Ministries and Messiah Biblical Institute, head pastor of Beth Messiah Congregation and an author. Michael Brown is Dean of Messiah Biblical Institute, an author, teacher and revivalist. Keith Intrater is pastor of El Shaddai Congregation, a Tikkun board member, an author and teacher. Andrew Shishkoff is also a pastor at Beth Messiah Congregation, a Tikkun board member and an evangelist. Jerry Miller is a pastor at Beth Messiah Congregation, a Tikkun board member and a teacher. Mikhael Murnane is the Director of Jerusalem Worship Dance, overseen by Tikkun board members.

The following pages list books available by our Tikkun leaders. Please use the form at the back of this book to place your order.

LAST DAYS TRILOGY

ISRAEL, THE CHURCH AND THE LAST DAYS

Must reading for all believers who want an exciting new perspective on the last days and the end-time role of Israel and the Church.
Price $9.95

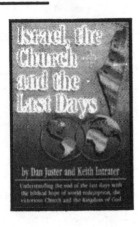

FROM IRAQ TO ARMAGEDDON

This book gives an in-depth analysis of end-time prophecy concerning the Middle East.
Price $7.95

REVELATION: THE PASSOVER KEY

An intriguing analysis explaining the similarities of the exodus from Egypt to the end times.
Price $6.95

MESSIANIC JEWISH THEMES

JEWISH ROOTS, A FOUNDATION OF BIBLICAL THEOLOGY
A significant book on Messianic Judaism which offers insight on many difficult questions.   **$10.00**

GROWING TO MATURITY, A MESSIANIC JEWISH GUIDE
This book is used by many congregations for membership classes.   **$9.00**

JEWISHNESS AND JESUS
A booklet to help you share Messiah with your unsaved Jewish friends.   **$1.00**

OUR HANDS ARE STAINED WITH BLOOD
For 1500 years the Church has persecuted the Jewish people. This shocking book exposes the roots of Christian anti-Semitism.   **$7.95**

OTHER BOOKS BY OUR AUTHORS

MICHAEL BROWN

HOW SAVED ARE WE?
An eye-opening book that will forever change our perspective on what it means to be a disciple of the Lord.   **$6.00**

THE END OF THE AMERICAN
GOSPEL ENTERPRISE

This urgent call for repentance exposes the bankrupt state of the American Church—and shows us the way to a real outpouring. **$6.00**

WHATEVER HAPPENED
TO THE POWER OF GOD?

This stirring book asks the questions you have always wanted to ask, and confronts you with answers that could change your life. **$7.95**

KEITH INTRATER

THE APPLE OF HIS EYE

Find out how your life can be transformed as you are bathed in the light of God's grace. **$6.00**

COVENANT RELATIONSHIPS

A handbook on the biblical principles of integrity and loyalty. This book lays important foundations for congregational health and right spiritual attitudes. **$12.00**

DAN JUSTER

DYNAMICS OF SPIRITUAL DECEPTION

This book will help you to avoid demonic counterfeit in Spirit-filled congregations. **$ 4.00**

ORDER FORM

LD101	ISRAEL, THE CHURCH AND THE LAST DAYS	$9.95
LD102	FROM IRAQ TO ARMAGEDDON	7.95
LD103	REVELATION: THE PASSOVER KEY	6.95
MJ201	JEWISH ROOTS	10.00
MJ202	GROWING TO MATURITY	9.00
MJ203	JEWISHNESS AND JESUS	1.00
MJ204	OUR HANDS ARE STAINED WITH BLOOD	7.95
AM301	HOW SAVED ARE WE?	6.00
AM302	THE END OF THE AMERICAN GOSPEL ENTERPRISE	6.00
AM303	WHATEVER HAPPENED TO THE POWER OF GOD?	7.95
AM304	THE APPLE OF HIS EYE	6.00
AM305	COVENANT RELATIONSHIPS	12.00
AM306	DYNAMICS OF SPIRITUAL DECEPTION	4.00

NAME_____ PHONE_____

ADDRESS_____

All items available to ministries and bookstores, in quantities of 5 or more, at 40% discount.

All orders must be prepaid.

ITEM	COST/BOOK	NO. ORDERED	AMOUNT

Subtotal _____

Maryland residents add 5% Sales Tax _____
(or send tax exempt certificate for our files)

15% P & H _____
($2.00 minimum)

TOTAL ENCLOSED _____

Mail all orders with checks payable to:
MBI Bookstore
13-15 E. Deer Park Drive, Suite 202
Gaithersburg, MD 20877

ORDER FORM

LD101	ISRAEL, THE CHURCH AND THE LAST DAYS	$9.95
LD102	FROM IRAQ TO ARMAGEDDON	7.95
LD103	REVELATION: THE PASSOVER KEY	6.95
MJ201	JEWISH ROOTS	10.00
MJ202	GROWING TO MATURITY	9.00
MJ203	JEWISHNESS AND JESUS	1.00
MJ204	OUR HANDS ARE STAINED WITH BLOOD	7.95
AM301	HOW SAVED ARE WE?	6.00
AM302	THE END OF THE AMERICAN GOSPEL ENTERPRISE	6.00
AM303	WHATEVER HAPPENED TO THE POWER OF GOD?	7.95
AM304	THE APPLE OF HIS EYE	6.00
AM305	COVENANT RELATIONSHIPS	12.00
AM306	DYNAMICS OF SPIRITUAL DECEPTION	4.00

NAME_____ PHONE_____

ADDRESS_____

_____

All items available to ministries and bookstores, in quantities of 5 or more, at 40% discount.

All orders must be prepaid.

ITEM	COST/BOOK	NO. ORDERED	AMOUNT

Subtotal _____

Maryland residents add 5% Sales Tax _____
(or send tax exempt certificate for our files)

15% P & H _____
($2.00 minimum)

TOTAL ENCLOSED _____

Mail all orders with checks payable to:
MBI Bookstore
13-15 E. Deer Park Drive, Suite 202
Gaithersburg, MD 20877